LEARNING FROM CHINA
A New Era of Retail Design

FRAME

CONTENTS

Buil
Comr

ding
munity

Boosting brand engagement through localisation and community-building strategies.

As e-commerce uproots the norms and conventions of physical retail – a trend that has been unmistakably accelerated by the COVID-19 crisis –, Chinese retailers are showing the way forward. This chapter gathers projects with a focus on establishing strong ties with customers by investing in localisation and community-building strategies. An inspiring variety of interpretations of this model shows us how brand loyalty can be promoted through retail spaces which give back to their communities – by contributing to the quality of shared urban spaces, and the day-to-day of customers, for example.

B.L.U.E. ARCHITECTURE STUDIO explores the full potential of a small-scale intervention to enhance the urban fabric

Eiichi Kano

Left An air conditioning system and air curtain machine at the entrance combine to control the indoor and outdoor air exchange.

Above The coffee shop's greenery connects to the Chinese parasol trees along the street, effectively furthering the idea of the interior as an extension of the street, and vice versa.

SHANGHAI - 'Coffee shops can do more than just serve coffee.' It was from this idea, and from a desire to explore an urban interface where the boundaries between inside and outside, private and public are put into question, that B.L.U.E.'s design for % Arabica came into being. The Beijing-based studio turned part of the shop's – private, money-making – interior into a park-like exterior, an addition to the city's shared social, public space that isn't directly profit-turning.

Located in a pedestrian-scale neighbourhood lined with historic architecture along West Jianguo Road, the transparent, welcoming design helps the coffee shop blend into the urban context and the streetscape. The team chose to leave the façade completely open by creating a small courtyard around a U-shaped glass box. A beautifully curved glass door that can be fully opened works in tandem with the cement coating continuous flooring to merge indoor and outdoor.

By transforming part of the 50-m² interior into an exterior, B.L.U.E. successfully designed the shop as an extension of the street. And while this meant decreasing the space's profit-making area, by improving the street and patrons' quality of life, the design is able to draw in more customers.

Left In a relatively small shop, the studio has generated public space where previously there was only a business.

Below The designers suggest that ideal city streets – and businesses – are those that generate chance encounters, and that the ideal urban interface blurs the boundary between inside and outside, private and public.

By transforming part of
the interior into an exterior,
B.L.U.E. successfully
designs a shop as an
extension of the street

LANDINI ASSOCIATES tailors a store format to local consumers for a retailer's entry into the Chinese market

Previous Spread Left Above the on-site cafeterias, which also incorporate the check-out counters, colourful ceiling murals are a playful hero graphics feature.

Previous Spread Right Lighting is designed to create a pleasant atmosphere and let the products speak, enhancing their colour, texture, and freshness.

Left In line with Landini Associates' design principles, there is no signage or ticketing displayed from the ceiling. Instead, category signage around the perimeter offers greater visibility across the stores and thus encourages cross-store shopping.

Right The team's messaging strategy was to highlight the quality and provenance of the products.

Andrew Meredith

SHANGHAI - Many retailers have crashed and burned on the Chinese discount market because China has already mastered this sector, itself. So, when tasked with creating two pilot stores for German-rooted supermarket chain ALDI in Shanghai, Sydney-based design agency Landini Associates worked closely with the client to thoroughly understand the local market.

Noticing that Chinese customers value quality and provenance, and prefer to visit multiple small, local retailers positioned for foot traffic, the team knew that the design needed to prioritise these qualities, while boldly expressing the ALDI brand in the busy Chinese food retail market. The resulting format and design is an evolution from the agency's work for the brand in Australia, with key differences in scale, layout and tone.

In the Shanghai stores, emphasis in given to key departments, including fresh produce, snacks, imported goods and health and beauty, with the most noticeable difference being the development of an on-site Food Station, as well as the addition of ready meals to take away or consume at the in-store dining kiosk.

The interiors are characterised by a palette of low cost but authentic materials such as locally sourced brick, terrazzo, an open concrete ceiling, warm timbers, and yellow accents, which add to the perception of freshness throughout. LED lighting reduces glare and running costs whilst improving ambience and colour rendering.

In tandem with the interiors, the team also designed an extensive series of signage and graphic illustrations that are entirely unique to the Chinese market. 'The use of imagery allows the stores to communicate language-free,' explains Landini Associates graphic design director Ben Goss, 'We could see that the use of an illustrative style paired with photography would work well and be a recognisable evolution of the ALDI Australia stores.' At the end of the customers' journey, a vibrant, colourful mural over the check-out counters captures the confidence and energy of what the brand has to offer.

CIFI SALES CENTER CHONGQING
IPPOLITO FLEITZ GROUP
establishes a dialogue between mankind and nature in an art gallery-like sales centre

CHONGQING – Young and lifestyle-oriented, millennials comprise China's most affluent demographic and they want it all: intensely urbane, they have a yen for the natural world too. On the mountainous outskirts of megacity Chongqing, a 1800-m² sales centre for real estate developer CiFi is as boldface as its clientele, and by embodying what they value, serves as a potent communication tool for the developer.

With its clear-glass frameless façade, the fulgent building by Ippolito Fleitz Group frames a gallery-like interior meant to be admired from the outside, but which can also admire the natural landscape from within. Both furniture and art echo the surrounding landscape in their form, structure and surface qualities, fostering a dialogue between nature and art.

While the design exudes a 'gracious spaciousness' and clarity, visitors are deliberately not allowed to view everything all at once in order to reveal the CiFi 'residential world' more intensely. A variety of design elements generate a strong sense of verticality while establishing zones that complement instead of competing with the strong architectonics of the building's arched walls and core.

The design team planned the lower floor to amplify brand and place, while the upper floor showcases the housing development itself. Linking the two, a dramatic floating staircase rises against a large vertical aluminium lighting wall. A central space under the circular core focuses attention on video projections and a large architectural model to showcase the property.

Previous Spread The glassy façades of the sales centre allow it to meld with the surrounding landscape, providing a bridge to nature, and a strong sense of the relationship between inside and outside, man and nature.

Left A dramatic floating staircase with terrazzo steps and a built-in glass railing is backgrounded by a vast vertical aluminium lighting wall feature.

Below The highly graphical ceiling consists of suspended chromed metal disks that give it a feeling of great depth.

Spencer Huang (Highlight Images)

This sales centre is as boldface as its clientele, and by embodying what they value, serves as a potent communication tool

Previous Spread A monumental circular core on the upper floor focuses visitors' attention on multimedia presentations.

Left The interior features a variety of design elements that establish a strong sense of verticality, including a graphical ceiling and tall metal curtains.

Above With sustainability in mind, the centre was designed such that, once the real estate sales phase is complete, the building will enjoy an afterlife as a restaurant or clubhouse.

Plan The sweeping building boasts an aerodynamic shape and a bold rounded core.

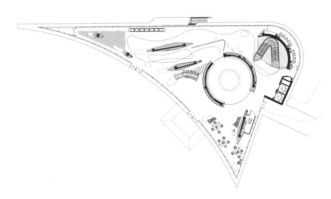

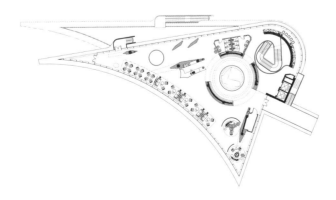

For a real estate sales centre, IPPOLITO FLEITZ GROUP immerses visitors in a relaxing ocean front lifestyle

QINGDAO - Its beachfront location was the inspiration for Ippolito Fleitz Group's design of real estate developer CiFi's 2400-m² sales centre. A showcase for luxe seaside living, the space emphasises a deep immersion in that lifestyle, with the interior design playing on the theme in a variety of ways.

From furniture to artworks, the property's proximity to the sea is emphasised on all floors. Guests begin on the second floor, where a low-ceiling room featuring a dozen photographs depicting ocean horizons introduces visitors to the theme. In an enclosed room, a sales presentation plays before low seating crafted from stylised hawsers. As the film ends, the screen-wall opens up, giving access to a balustrade with an ocean view.

A sculptural staircase leads down to the first floor, which hosts a large-scale architectural model of the property, a VIP room, more views and a lounge bar for sales discussions. From here, a lift runs to the ground floor where, in the cafeteria, the maritime mood is amplified by the use of transparent blues and shiny silver tones. This space exemplifies the arc of the interior design, from clear, open areas to dense zones with haptic qualities that serve as a condensed showcase for luxury ocean living.

Built with adaptive reuse in mind, the centre can be repurposed as a restaurant with minimal construction when the sales phase of the project is complete.

Previous Spread The team created a sales centre for a luxury seaside property development that immerses visitors in a maritime mood.

Left The designers highlighted the development's proximity to water in both subtle and direct ways, from fin-like aluminium lamella to rippling steel panel ceilings and generous fields of aqua blue glass walls.

Above On the second level, a gallery-like room displays a dozen photographs of ocean horizons.

Right On the top floor, where visitors start their journey, a sales presentation plays in a small cinema furnished with low seats crafted from stylised hawsers.

Fenfang Lu

From furniture to artworks, the property's proximity to the sea is emphasised on all floors

Below The customer journey ends in the ground floor cafeteria, where the designers condensed the maritime mood through the use of transparent blues and shiny silver tones.

Right The designers gave the sales centre an open, flowing character and an atmospheric but subdued colour palette: black, white and grey are accented with pale wood, aqua blue glass and mineral hues.

Plan The rich layout varies from densely concentrated areas to more spacious zones.

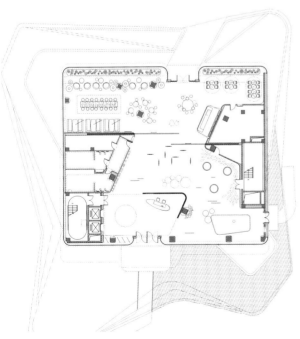

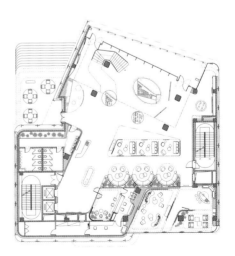

CRASH BAGGAGE

ALBERTO CAIOLA channels one single, bold narrative to connect a brand to its own tribe

SHANGHAI – Italian luggage brand Crash Baggage specialises in deliberately dented, seemingly damaged suitcases which encourage customers to be carefree in their travels. In line with its adventurous spirit, Italian designer Alberto Caiola created an immersive spatial experience for the brand's Shanghai launch. The installation took visitors on a journey to fantastical frontiers, far from earthly concerns about lost luggage, travel logistics – and even gravity.

Through a playful temporary space and single bold narrative, Caiola committed the 'outlaw' baggage brand to engage its actual clientele instead of trying to appeal to just anyone walking in off the street. Of course, the unconventional space was so playful, it may just have done that, too.

Occupying 110 m² in the department store, the interior invited the brand's target demographic – young, footloose and trendy – to leave convention at the door. A bright, monolithically yellow space was anchored by a solitary model pedalling a stationary exercise bike while towing a lunar buggy piled with Crash Baggage's signature suitcases and wrapped in hazard tape. In this other-worldly destination, even movement became nonsensical, with the traveller's progress measured not by distance, but by a moving LED backdrop. Extreme and surreal, the installation effectively broadcast Crash Baggage's reputation for manufacturing durable products in highly resistant materials, capable of withstanding the harshest, or even most far-fetched, conditions.

Dirk Weiblen

Previous Spread An immersive installation highlights the value of exploring more and worrying less.

Left To emphasise adventure, the all-yellow space is anchored by a sculptural installation.

Right At the brand's Shanghai debut, a DJ played next to oversize disco balls in the shop's storage room to illustrate the products' capaciousness, durability and free spirit.

Next Spread The design focuses on the brand's actual customers, in order to cultivate a deeper, more emotional engagement.

Through the installation's bold narrative, Caiola committed the brand to engage its actual clientele and in doing so, sparked the curiosity of a larger audience

NONG STUDIO uses a modern approach to dig into a brand's local roots

Chasing Wang

Left Reclaimed dark-grey bricks clad the store's entryway.

Above A mirror-clad wall adds dimension to the interior.

SHANGHAI – Behind the exclusive and overbearing entrance to a shopping mall, the first brick-and-mortar store for women's fashion label Eva Essential features an interior washed in compelling contrasts.

Local firm Nong Studio set a pink glass door into a transparent glass storefront. This rose-coloured portal leads into a vestibule lined with reclaimed dark-grey bricks. Materials like the bricks were chosen in order to articulate the brand's local origins. The architects even preserved certain elements commonly found in the classic Shanghai stores of yore, including large light wells (actually created here using luminous LED film lighting). 'Grey concrete tile flooring punctuated with blond timber plank, and vintage garment poles installed on the walls are all meant to exude a local memory,' the design team explains.

In a boutique that embodies a meeting of East and West, past and future, light toned finishes and décor stand in contrast with the aforementioned elements. This lighter palette is intended to denote the brand's connection to a chic and casual lifestyle. A backdrop of pale-beige plaster walls is dotted with golden brass elements and mirror, both of which add dimension to the 180-m² interior.

LITTLE H

DAYLAB proposes a new role for physical retail

Left In an era when mobile technology and e-commerce are mainstream, what form should the new retail space assume? Daylab tries to answer this question in the design of the Little H boutique.

Above Daylab created a 'secret garden', dividing rooms like plant beds and using curved walls to organise the space.

BEIJING – Located on the 31st floor of an office building rather than on the high street or in a shopping mall, this 90-m² luxury fashion boutique has its roots in e-commerce. The bulk of Little H customers no longer need to buy from the physical shop, but for those wishing to shop in person, this space welcomes visitors and features displays that lend themselves to product shoots and online webcasting. Daylab dubbed it an 'office store' and used its unusual location as a springboard for design.

The team mapped out a 'secret garden', boldly dividing the space into various zones, giving each a theme and hiding discoverable details that merit exploration. The space is interspersed by curved panels which create several niches, each containing its own particular scenography. This solution ensures that the lack of clear sightlines and openness, which would be a problem in traditional shops, becomes a virtue in the office store.

The space functions at once as a retail floor, an afternoon tea salon, a background for vlogging, and a private studio. In the era of e-commerce, in what format can physical retail exist? As the design team puts it, 'Little H is one attempt at a possible answer.'

Below The boutique combines several programmes in one space: a fashion retail floor, an afternoon tea salon, a canvas for vlogging, and a private studio.

Right Cradled between curved walls and with amorphous cut-outs for doors, each room features its own look and feel.

Yuuuun Studio

In the era of e-commerce,
in what format can physical
retail exist? Little H is one
attempt at a possible answer

ANYSCALE creates a unique retail space by reducing design to its essence

Left The bespoke display wall cleverly combines product display with storage for the small shop's inventory.

Above In its context at the Uni_Joy space in the Joy City mall, the all-white shop, with its limited range of materials, lets the products, themselves, attract and engage passers-by.

Next Spread The brand wanted a small-scale store that was clearly related to its original flagship but at the same time condensed, distinct and surprising in its own right.

BEIJING – Polyphony, a lifestyle retailer selling comics and character figurines, asked Anyscale Achitecture Design to condense its successful flagship, also designed by the local studio, into 70 m² whilst making it distinct and unexpected. The result is a sister store that has been skilfully 'reduced to the max'.

A compact footprint challenged the designers to streamline the retail experience: to engage and surprise customers immediately and to store and display products in a single place. The team focused on how to integrate product displays by creating a custom-designed signature wall with half-moon acrylic windows embedded in drawers that contain the products.

They sourced high-precision hinges for the drawer-displays and used LED lights to illuminate them seamlessly and without any glare.

'With a focus on physical retail in a digital world, Polyphony's Artemis attracts customers through its specific buying experience,' the designers explain. Customers can reach into the displays to pick out products themselves, a close handling of the merchandise which helps create a sense of connection and ownership.

All told, designing at a small scale allowed Anyscale to reduce the interior concept to the essential. And by limiting its material palette and finishes, enable the products to sell themselves.

'With a focus on physical retail in a digital world, Polyphony's Artemis attracts customers through its specific buying experience'

Sensor Images

KOKAISTUDIOS reintegrates a mall into the fabric and life of the city

Left and Above Effectively circumnavigating the mall proper, a theatrical 'red carpet', primarily for tourists, offers impressive views across East Nanjing Road and People's Square.

Left The re-design – including decanting a street-level entrance into a handsome wood-flanked atrium – imagines Shanghai residents as the 'audience' and repositions the mall as a lifestyle destination that extends beyond retail.

Right and Next Spread The heart of the mall, envisaged as a 'backstage' space for local office workers, feels industrial but posh with its grey louver walls and sleek black fields of glass.

Elevation By reconfiguring and clarifying circulation inside and outside, Kokaistudios made it possible for the mall to reanimate the urban fabric around it.

Wu Qingshan

SHANGHAI – Local architecture and interior design firm Kokaistudios 'upgraded' the existing retail components of the 58,000-m² Shimao Festival City shopping centre. At the same time, by reconfiguring circulation inside and outside and identifying clear pathways for different visitor types, the designers enabled the mall to reinvigorate its surroundings and this way reconnect with the city as a 'useful public space of engagement and exchange'.

The conceptual model for the mall's renovation was a theatre and focused on the roles played by three types of protagonists or patrons: tourists, 'audience members' and 'actors', who populate the 'foyer', 'auditorium' and 'backstage'. Starting outside, an external 'red carpet' guides tourists along a sky escalator on an experiential journey that circumnav-

igates the mall and its big views, reactivating upper levels. Shanghai residents are the mall's 'audience' for whom it becomes a lifestyle destination beyond its commercial purpose. They use a street-level entrance into an attractive wood slat-flanked atrium that extends the mall's height to make it light, open and dramatic. Another entrance caters to 'actors', visitors who work in nearby offices, who are conveyed on an escalator directly to the heart of the mall, a 'backstage' area with a swank but industrial look: grey louver walls and polished black glass.

The project illustrates the ideal that architectural renovation of certain properties can also serve cities, as a whole, by retrofitting outdated spaces to suit current lifestyles, and making them more flexible in the future.

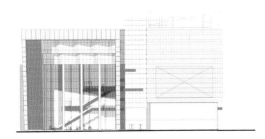

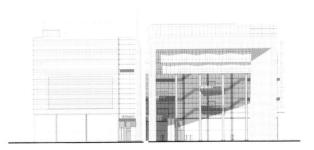

TEMPORARY SITE OF SHENGLI MARKET

For a temporary market site, LUO STUDIO uses modular, recyclable components, ensuring a speedy and sustainable construction

Jin Weiqi

PUYANG – Located in a dilapidated urban area, Shengli Market needed a temporary location from which to serve the local population while the old quarter is being rehabilitated. Beijing-based Luo Studio was tapped to design the market's temporary site.

The solution – a fully industrialised greenhouse-like structure built with standardised, lightweight, modular, prefabricated and recyclable or reusable components – allowed for quick construction on a low budget. But it also improved the shopping and selling experiences of the market's users and ensured that the temporary structure's materials can be repurposed when the market's new, permanent location opens.

While the interiors of most traditional food markets are visually chaotic; Luo Studio's design establishes order and keeps sightlines open through the installation of a series of enclosed shops along the perimeter and open shelves in the centre of the space. The dimensions of each of the larger, three-sided, 4x4-m perimeter shops are coordinated with the sizes of the external walls' standardised structural rods. In the 'shelf' area, one booth occupies 2x2-m shelves. Further aiding good visibility, inverted rectangular pyramids carry LED lighting fixtures and signage.

Materials consist primarily of ordinary, easy-to-install-and-disassemble timber, lightweight steel panels, cement slabs, steel angles and polycarbonate sheets. The organic warmth and ubiquity of the timber throughout establishes a strong visual identity and a sense of order. It also allows the colours and textures of the produce to sell themselves.

Previous Spread At the entrance, a canopy is built out of rectangular pyramid structures which ensure both stability of construction and economy of materials.

Left Natural and warm-coloured timber was applied to the open counters, cornices of the enclosed shops and umbrella-shaped structural columns, thereby resulting in a clear visual identity.

Above Because it was not feasible to place signage on the booths, the team affixed inverted rectangular pyramid structures onto the space's structural columns. These steel and timber structures not only host wayfinding and vendor information, but also the light installations.

While the interiors of most traditional food markets are visually chaotic, Luo Studio's design establishes order and keeps sightlines open

THE NORTH FACE BASECAMP

COORDINATION ASIA's boldface visuals guide shoppers into the realms – and lifestyle – of the explorer

CHONGLI - More than just a retail space, The North Face's 175-m² Basecamp store is a place that welcomes a like-minded community of alpine 'explorers'. Designed by Shanghai-based studio Coordination Asia, the interior, much like a basecamp, adapts to various events and activities, as needed.

An extensive LED light structure of The North Face logo frames an oft-changing 'semi-pop-up' area at the front. Three rows of black and white wooden benches behind the logo serve as a community space and rest area accommodating up to 26 people. Opposite, the 'Warm up Lounge' featuring a bar counter which extends from the store's interior invites customers to relax and swap stories over hot drinks.

Inside, a brand wall consisting of woodblocks mimicking the iconic Half Dome element of the brand's logo serves as backdrop for store displays as well as a 'sweet spot for social media posts'. Above the central display, which is made up of a series of terrain simulation platforms, a neon light sculpture traces the ridge lines of a mountain, a nod to the store's location at a ski resort.

The corner rest area features a pair of chairs covered in yellow fabric recycled from The North Face's legendary tent reflecting the brand's efforts to promote a sustainable lifestyle. The bright colours and soft materials here complement the rougher materials and textures elsewhere, including aluminium furniture, wooden walls and the dark grey stone-like floor tiles.

Charlie Xia

Previous Spread Framed by a large LED structure, a semi-pop-up area serves as the starting point where explorers can prepare themselves for any adventure.

Left Light installations and boulder bases for mannequins allude to the geography of the store's location at a ski resort.

Above A brand wall with Half Dome-shaped wooden sculptures inspired by the logo pays tribute to the brand's heritage.

Next Spread The store translates the explorer's spirit of adventure into a versatile space hosting events and activities, such as lectures, film screenings and training programmes.

Like a basecamp, the interior adapts to various events and activities, as needed

KEY TAKEAWAYS

By finding creative ways of contributing to patrons' day-to-day quality of life – for example, giving back space to a community – brands and businesses have the opportunity of creating stronger ties with customers, thus building brand loyalty.

Architectural renovation and rehabilitation of certain properties can also serve cities, as a whole. By expanding the functionality and reconsidering circulation of large-scale retail outlets, these structures can be reabsorbed into the city as useful public spaces of engagement and exchange.

Built with adaptive reuse in mind, temporary retail spaces like sales centres can be repurposed as hospitality or cultural venues, remaining an important part of the community.

In a highly competitive market, diligently studying the local market and responding to the values, habits and culture of local consumers in every detail of design can be the difference between a brand's success and downfall.

By eschewing one-size-fits-all solutions and instead engaging a brand's specific target audience, retail spaces may just find the creative solutions needed to appeal to a wider pool of consumers.

Destir
Re

ation:
ail

Boosting brand engagement through multifunctional lifestyle destinations.

New Retail, Online-Merge-Offline, Phygital Retail... The labels are plentiful, but they all stem from one simple observation: the future of retail is in clever combinations of online and in-shop experiences. Just as there are many names for this model, there are even more iterations of how it can be applied. The projects in this chapter aren't all examples of 'new retail', but rather of one of the ways in which physical retail can not only complement, but also reinforce e-commerce: the ever more popular interpretation of retail space as a destination.

BEAST AND LITTLE B
SÒ STUDIO turns Josef Albers' two-dimensional colour studies into three-dimensional space

Hongbin Wang Linshan Film

Left A spiral staircase in Beast transitions from the avant-garde ground floor into a Tuscan fairyland upstairs.

Above Layered glass and gradients of colour reinterpret Hard-edge art in three dimensions and represent the distinction and the bond between two sister stores, Beast and Little B.

BEIJING – The façade of dual-brand store Beast and Little B in the Taikoo Li Sanlitun shopping centre was inspired by American Hard-edge artist Josef Albers and the reinterpretation of his two-dimensional colour studies into three-dimensional space. The façade looks both soft and hard, uniform and hierarchical, grading from purple to pink before arriving at Little B's ginger yellow tones. The progression of colour between the two stores distinguishes the two brands, while allowing them to share modern 'genes'.

Inside the 245-m² space, designed by Sò Studio, two floors represent a gradient of stylistic eras. The first floor takes up the avant-garde

language of the façade. Its jewellery area grades from bold pink to purple and juxtaposes contrasts of material and age, coarseness and polish: There are adjacent stone and metal surfaces and an old wooden fireplace displayed in a sleek glass tube.

A coffee area on the second floor borrows from the past. In contrast to the floor below, it appears elegant, classical and calm, while incorporating several surreal elements. The process of going up the stairs becomes an interstitial moment, leading from a modern space into a seemingly parallel universe, embedded in the nostalgia of the past.

Left Illuminated, Little B's glass façade, layered with glowing additive colour, looks like a luminous box floating in air, making it the focal point of the street.

Below An existing partition wall between the two stores was opened, allowing patrons to circulate between the two.

The progression of colour between the two stores distinguishes the two brands

CONEMOTING MARKET

YEBIN DESIGN creates an offline destination as an extension of a brand's online presence

Above The basement retail space has 5-m-high ceilings and a playfully sculptural look.

SHENZHEN – With the entrenchment of our lives online, physical stores have evolved from sales spaces into a social milieux and increasingly complex expressions of lifestyle. Conemoting Market is a reflection of this tectonic shift: It doesn't just display and sell goods. It is an offline space designed in the service of the virtual.

The project, by Hangzhou-based studio Yebin, involved the renovation and transformation of a 1990s residential building, not only into a shop, but also – and perhaps more importantly – a social space for a new generation of consumers. Its basement, with 5-m-high ceilings, serves as a retail space, displaying garments and select products by independent brands, whilst the ground floor is a café by day and a bar at night.

Sculptural, scenographic and photogenic, the ground floor dining area is sharply divided by red and orange tempered glass, establishing a somewhat psychedelic visual experience, and creating a sharp contrast between indoor and outdoor.

Underground, white metal paint highlights the store's display and acts as a background for photo-taking. The retail space, which the design team describes as having 'an upscale industrial art atmosphere', is wrapped in metallic silver, and features a series of bespoke display and decorative elements, including large white blocks punctuated with plaster busts and bound with slender red nylon straps, huge glossy spheres of varying dimensions, and a metal giraffe sculpture that penetrates two floors: its face pops up in the café whilst its feet stand in the basement.

Yebin hopes that this 580-m² destination will pave the way for future retail and renovation projects in the neighbourhood.

Below The warm glow of the ground floor's coloured glass divisions is reinforced by its contrast with the building's cold silver façade, making the space stand out on the street.

Right A giant metal giraffe sculpture rises from the basement retail area through to the ground floor's café, hinting at the playful interiors below.

Xiaoyun

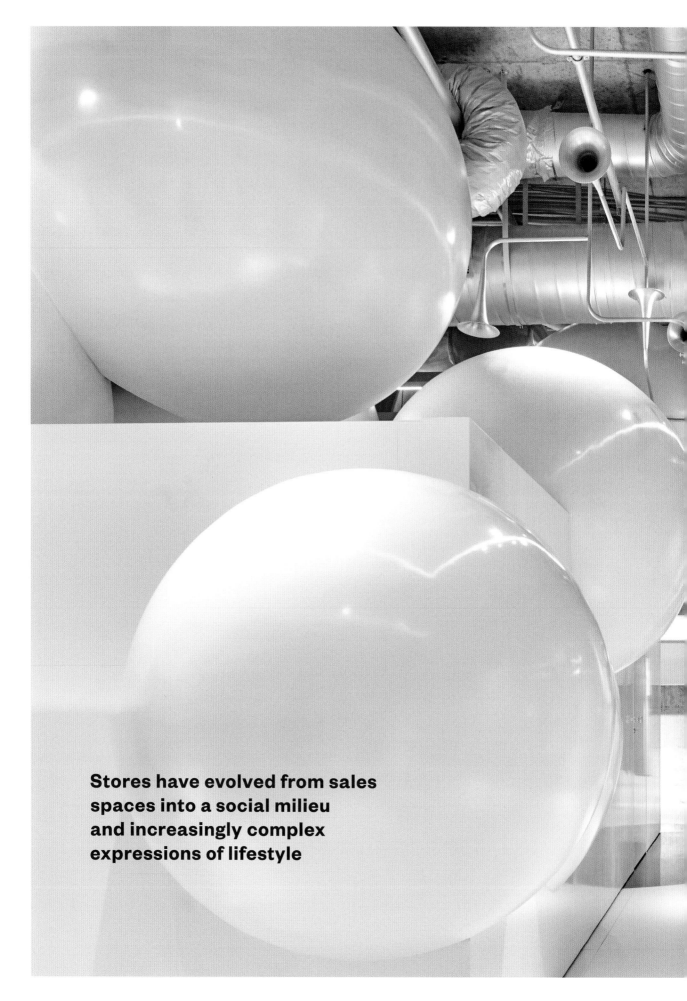

Stores have evolved from sales
spaces into a social milieu
and increasingly complex
expressions of lifestyle

Previous Spread Red, silver and gold accents enrich the vastly white landscape of the retail floor.

Left A plethora of unusual displays adorn the retail area, creating plenty of photo ops and contributing to the space's identity as a destination.

Right Pop Art-like, red teddy bears support large iridescent display boxes.

Diagram The neighbourhood's first concept store featuring a café and bar, Conemoting Market is set to establish a model for future renovation projects in the community.

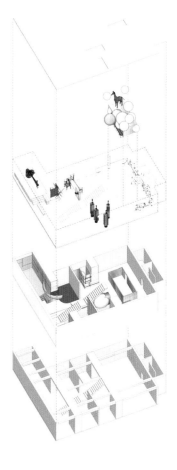

Left Thick arches across the open-plan space evoke classical Italian porticos and are suggestive of socialising and cultural exchange.

Above Postmodern geometric stand-alone displays function as landmarks in the surreal landscape.

HARBOOK

In a digital era, ALBERTO CAIOLA designs an ode to the printed page

HANGZHOU - In a Chinese city that has been home to writers, philosophers and poets of legend, Harbook wears its heritage with a progressive spirit, mixing lifestyle elements into its retail space to draw in a new generation of city-dwellers. The 600-m² bookstore, café, and contemporary Scandinavian furniture show-room, is a model that blends tradition with aspiration.

Like a landscape in a Surrealist painting, the space abstracts an urban environment – arches, columns, an indoor sky – as a provocation to the imagination. Extending across an other-wise open-plan space, a series of thick arches evokes the classical Italian portico, an element long associated across eras and cultures with socialising, cultural exchange, shopping and dining. To emphasise this cityscape, stand-alone geometric displays embellish the space like abstract sculptures and the luminous ceiling is gridded with Barrisol.

The colour scheme – dusty pink, timeworn industrial concrete, silver and black – and an unconventional mixture of materials co-exist with more classical elements. A custom staircase ascends to a raised café area floored with locally sourced grey brick, a nod to the local context in an otherwise culturally neutral environment. Overhead, a LED light installation serves as both a dramatic centrepiece and a metaphor for the enlightenment contained in books – as opposed to the more literal and ubiquitous illu-mination of digital screens.

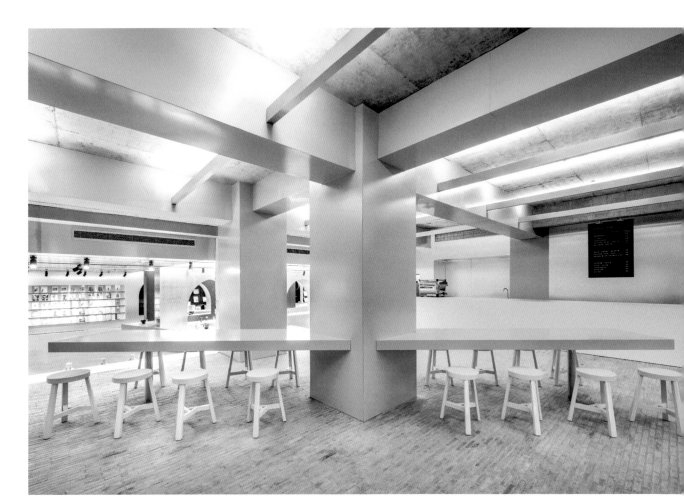

Left The design mixes materials and colours unconventionally, using a colour scheme that ranges from dusty pink, purple and green to silver and black.

Right The shop, which will sell both books and furniture, hosts readers and furniture display on tiered platforms.

Next Spread The interior resembles an abstracted Surrealist landscape and is meant to accommodate a mixture of retail types.

A LED light installation serves as a dramatic centrepiece and a metaphor for the enlightenment contained in books

Left The store's extreme flexibility, vis-à-vis contents and theme, is enabled by such things as scaffolding-like stainless steel display racks, which can be changed depending on the products showcased.

Below Heyshop 2.0 integrates multiple business formats across day and night, whilst merging the brand's on and offline shopping experiences.

HEYSHOP 2.0

DAYLAB unifies four business models into a single space, allowing them not only to coexist, but reinforce each other

SHANGHAI – For its second brick-and-mortar location, e-commerce platform Heyshop tasked design studio Daylab (who also authored the brand's first physical store) with integrating not only multiple brands, but also different commercial formats into a cohesive space. Heyshop 2.0 brings together retail space, a café, bar and photo studio into a single store, enabling it to change from day into night mode, and successfully expressing the designers' vision of 'new retail': Online-Merge-Offline (OMO).

Lack of space, varying business hours or tangled circulation can limit the success of a multi-format layout in one store. Daylab, however, organised the 560-m² space so that the formats complete one another, instead of competing with each other. For example, whereas stand-alone photo studios must provide makeup services and dressing rooms, in Heyshop 2.0 these functions are already available via the fitting room, makeup tables and accessories of the adjacent retail space.

Another key design strategy sees the large dressing room enriching both the offline and online brand experience: while offering visitors different seasonal scenarios and décor, it also provides the perfect livestreaming background for the brand's taste-making clientele, augmenting its online exposure.

Finally, looking to maximise the brand's profit and the customers' pleasure, the café turns into a night-time bar. As the designers put it, 'Heyshop is no longer just a 12-hour store, but a 24-hour hot spot.'

Left Hanging LED display screens can rapidly indicate a change of brand or product category, supporting rapid reconfiguration of the space.

Right The décor of the dressing room will change over the course of seasons, offering an important livestreaming setting for clients.

Yuuuun Studio

FITTING ROOM

④ ⑤ ⑥ ⑦ ⑧ ⑨ ⑩

YI MOMENT PH

Daylab organised the space so that different commercial formats complete one another, instead of competing with each other

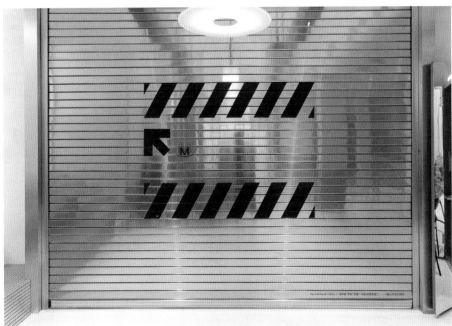

Left Bar and coffee shop can share the same space because one opens when the other closes and they use almost the same furnishings.

Right Simply pulling down shutters at certain points can close off retail at its day's end, whilst still offering night-time access to the bar area.

NORMAL²AB

SIMPLE SPACE DESIGN
blurs the boundaries of architectural and interior elements to create a richer experience of space

ZHONGSHAN – Reborn from a disused factory, the 365-m² Normal²ab accommodates work space for photographers, designers and floral artists, as well as a café. A box-in-box composition animates the façade and creates a fluid relationship between the business and the residential neighbourhood where it is located.

Jutting forward from the original façade, these boxes naturally form two recessed entryways. The main entrance, landscaped like a courtyard, features a black overhang and a tall wooden door whose glazed handles – one black, another transparent – are meant to entice visitors to explore the interior. Standing in contrast, a smaller white box, features floor-to-ceiling glazed openings, establishing a strong connection between interior and exterior.

Inside, the space contains an expectant, easily fillable emptiness. Light flows in, tattooing the white walls of the ground level with shadows that 'move like an hour hand in space', altering the atmosphere of the interior according to time of day and weather. This 'blank canvas' floor serves as an open, reconfigurable space for dining and events. A graphical black line runs across the rear wall, sister to the overhang outside, containing a staircase with black and white steps that lead up to a first floor design atelier.

By blurring the boundaries of architectural and interior elements – a window is also a room, stair platforms look like stacked building blocks, a windowsill functions as a counter – local studio Simple Space Design looked to create a richer experience of space. Both the designers and the owners hope that the commercial success of Normal²ab will inspire the city to see the potential in renovating and rehabilitating its old buildings, instead of building anew.

Previous Spread The design allows sunlight to pour through doors and windows, altering the look and feel of the space depending on time and weather.

Below Taking over an old factory, Normal²ab integrates event space and workspace for photographers, designers, floral artists and caterers.

Right The white ground floor is an open flexible space that, up a black and white staircase, turns into a studio and design work area.

Little Praise

For a co-retail space, STUDIO DOHO tucks a reconfigurable interior behind a capturing, brand-defining storefront

SHANGHAI – Brick-and-mortar retail is changing precipitously around the globe, but perhaps nowhere faster than in China. The rise of online shopping has forced brands and designers to re-imagine traditional shopping in the form of disruptive formats. An example is OceanSpot, a co-retail start-up that curates shopping experiences based on themes.

The brand's first concept store in Shanghai needed to make a bold statement to attract customers whilst accommodating a variety of rapidly changing product displays. Local firm Studio DOHO covered the exterior of the double-height, 127-m² storefront with a curved, colour-changing dichroic film that establishes a strong brand identity and a destination business on the street.

The film casts shifting, colourful 'light shadows' on the surrounding kerb and features circular cut-outs that open up areas for storefront merchandising.

While the façade establishes the house brand outside, an ever-changing interior pushes the envelope – and elasticity – of traditional brick-and-mortar retail. A custom grid system made from wood and metal was mounted to walls and columns, accommodating a dynamic, highly changeable setting for multiple emerging brands with diverse products, both large and small. A bespoke shelf and hook system holds countless combinations, while serving as a handsome and distinctive wallcovering.

An ever-changing interior pushes the envelope – and elasticity – of traditional brick-and-mortar retail

Previous Spread Left OceanSpot's distinctive façade is veiled with curved colour-shifting dichroic film to establish a bold brand identity and a destination retail space.

Previous Spread Right A custom grid system made from wood and metal was mounted to walls and columns, allowing rapid changes of display.

Left The space also hosts a craft coffee bar to unite creative professionals working in the complex and a showroom for premium wood supplier Fiemme.

Right The branded exterior finds its counterpoint in a highly creative but, in a sense, blank interior, allowing the space's curators to work with diverse brands and products, large and small.

Seth Powers Photography

ONMYOJI THEME STORE

E STUDIO uses light as a design material, turning an interior into a beacon for gamers around the globe

GUANGZHOU – More than 200 million people around the world have downloaded Onmyoji, a turn-based fantasy strategy game developed by NetEase. Set during the Heian period, the story follows an *onmyoji*, or ghost, who bridges the human and spirit worlds, on a quest for his lost memories. As the company's first offline theme store, the 385-m² restaurant, exhibition space and flagship had to represent beloved historical game elements within a wholly modern interior. The design included a renovation that would create a series of 'experience spaces' – a café, bar, retail floor and showroom – that entertain and engage young people with both the game and other gamers.

The polycarbonate façade of the layered building turn it into a luminous lantern. Distinct from its wooded surroundings and representing parts of the game's narrative, the building serves as a filter, producing various visual effects through the manipulation of light. The Courtyard of the Onmyojis was inspired by *karesansui*, the Japanese rock garden. Its plan starts with a rippling pattern that spreads outward, so that the layout of the courtyard ripples and creases upward in the form of stairs to reach the upper level. At night, via carefully controlled illumination, the first floor café transforms into a bar. During the day, however, sunlight cascading through the surrounding trees onto the polycarbonate walls bathes the space in a filigree of light and shadows.

Chao Zhang

Previous Spread NetEase's first offline concept flagship, Onmyoji is a lightbox that supports quickly changing visual themes from the brand's most popular games.

Left Memes from the Onmyoji storyline are rendered on the mesh walls that enclose a series of semi-private spaces, illuminated in a variety of ways to express the competition at the heart of the game.

Above Gaps in the wooden elements around the sheer polycarbonate walls emphasise the rhythm of the architecture.

Right The Courtyard of the Onmyojis was influenced by the Japanese concept of the 'dry landscape', or rock garden.

Diagram The plan starts with a rippling pattern that spreads outward, so that the courtyard ripples and creases upward in the form of stairs to reach an upper level.

Woods
Stone
Stairs

Retail meets hospitality meets work in a thoughtful renovation project by MUUA DESIGN STUDIO

Previous Spread An enclosed central courtyard serves as the entrance to the building and buffers its mixed programmes while bringing much-needed light inside.

Left Top The renovation of a mid-century granary and its interiors involved preserving some original features and materials and creating a collage of diverse interiors to serve its many functions.

Left Bottom A concrete passage marks the entrance to the retail space.

Right Opposite the two-room guest-house, the commercial area of the building features an extended bar clad in green and white tiles, as well as a variety of vintage furniture and decorations, all of which can be purchased by guests.

Yujie Liu

HUZHOU – Local hospitality and culture brand PlanChum tasked Muua Design Studio with the rehabilitation of a 1950s-era granary building into a multi-industry store. The 600-m² space's unusual mix of programmes brings together a showcase of vintage products and plants (all available for sale), a restaurant serving light fare, work and event space, and a two-room guesthouse.

Given its original functions and age, the old granary was dark and had a leaky roof. The design team decided to rebuild the latter, while preserving its form and original terracotta tiles. A new steel structure now supports the roof, which integrates glazed openings at strategic points, allowing plenty of natural light to flood the interiors.

Marking PlanChum Yucun's entrance is a central enclosed courtyard anchored by a large osmanthus tree. The courtyard brings the outdoors inside and serves as a quiet buffer between the guesthouse on the building's south side and the multifunctional retail space on the north. The latter is organised into a ground floor and mezzanine, enlarging the usable square footage and deepening the sense of hierarchy and variegation throughout the interiors.

Muua's thoughtful renovation and material selection – combining red bricks, soft wooden elements, and vintage furniture with open spaces, blank walls and sleek green tiles – successfully expresses both the building's memory, and its current use.

Left On the courtyard's south side, a distinctive asymmetrical red brick wall leads into the boutique accommodation.

Right For the guesthouse, the design team selected earthy materials, including wood, textiles and leather in subdued tones, hoping to create a comfortable and relaxed environment.

The courtyard brings the outdoors in and serves as a quiet buffer between the building's various programmes

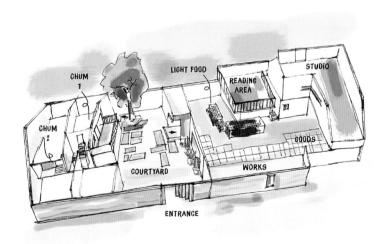

RÅ SPACE imports a 'soft futurism' from Scandinavia to China in the form of its own store

Rå Space

Left and Above In Danish, Råhuset translates roughly to 'the undecorated house'.

CHANGZHOU – After studying in Milan and Copenhagen, and working for the likes of LEGO, NASA, B&B, Riva1920 and smaller studios, Seamus Wang and Esben Yan established their own office in China. The duo quickly decided that the region's furniture industry was blighted with a wilting uniformity and that this sameness was leaving consumers with what they described as aesthetic fatigue.

When the two decided to open their own design showroom and to design it themselves, they envisioned Råhuset – Danish for 'the undecorated house' – as a hybrid of the creative and commercial, a place where they could offer furniture from a variety of well-known Nordic brands, but also an experimental art space that could inspire locals to better understand the value and potential of design.

The duo injected Råhuset with the typical warmth and hygge, or cosiness, of Scandinavian culture, but also added doses of intense colour and fields of cooler, coarser materials like steel, granite and roughly textured coated concrete. They reconfigure the 228-m² shop periodically, altering anything from furniture placement and lighting to shelving according to changing themes. The space is meant to embody the values of Nordic furniture, using its own shifting character to suggest that home décor is also self-expression, an intimate form of personal branding.

Left Rough granite floors and concrete walls serve as a neutral backdrop to the space's ever-changing displays.

Below Stainless steel LED tubes and spotlights mounted on a track lighting system confer plenty of adaptability to the instore lighting.

The space's shifting character suggests that home décor is also self-expression

Left Leading to a small first-floor office space, a blue coated steel staircase doubles as an eye-catching display.

Above Stainless steel partitions, displays and shelving feature prominently throughout, contributing to the desired futuristic interior.

KOKAISTUDIOS redefines Shanghai's lifestyle retail with an immersive and evolving environment

Left The venue is organised into functional areas conceived as gardens and arranged thematically by season.

Above The second floor autumn garden features a reconfigurable seating arrangement that can serve various functions.

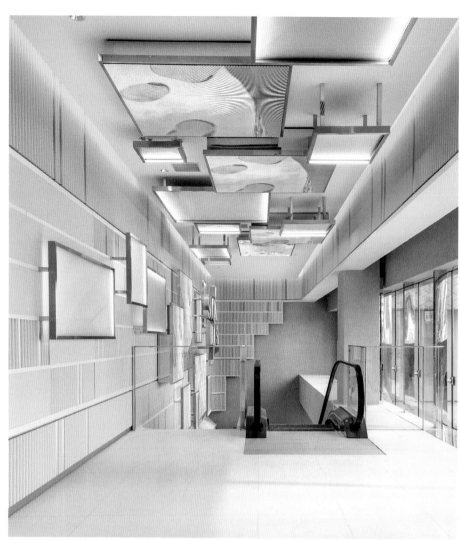

Left The design seeks to bring the vitality of the city inside, with escalators flanked by audiovisual installations broadcasting abstracted spring flowers and clouds.

Right and Diagram A silo of bookshelves draws visitors to the upper level via a spiral staircase encased within.

SHANGHAI – Social House by Xintiandi is a multifunctional emporium that synthesises retail, F&B and lifestyle elements. Occupying 4000-m^2 across two floors, the space was designed to cultivate openness and exchange, and to draw the energy of the urban fabric inside. Local firm Kokaistudios crafted the interior narrative around circulation and flow, punctuating it with focal points of activity, and making it a perennially evolving destination.

To connect to its outside environment and convey the cyclical nature of its changing programmes of pop-ups, exhibitions and events, the design team organised the space into seasonal 'gardens'. The retail platform is in the spring garden: colourful and spacious, it hosts fashion, style and beauty pop-up shops. The summer garden focuses on nourishment for body and mind, with a cookery school, teahouse and travel photography gallery.

The second floor autumn garden sits atop a spiral staircase within a silo of bookshelves, with a flexible seating arrangement that can serve as anything from a day-lit lounge or cosy reading nook to a casual meeting space or book-themed event space. The winter garden continues the outside-in journey with its focus on wellbeing in the form of a gym and open kitchen that hosts visiting chefs. Layered within this, seven unique pavilions extend the garden metaphor, designed to hold changing content and lending the space an extra 'ecosystem' of functionality.

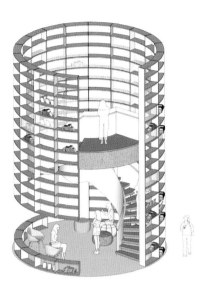

To connect to its outside environment and convey the cyclical nature of its changing programmes, the space is organised into seasonal 'gardens'

RAMOPRIMO's interior for
a multi-brand store and event
space has the flow and sheen
of a garment in motion

Marcella Campa

Previous Spread This multifunctional flagship looks to provide a social and creative space where fashion lovers can come together for events and exhibitions.

Left In the entrance area, a rotating room functions as a stage for the work of young Chinese fashion designers.

SHENYANG – A multifunctional meeting place for denizens of the fashion industry, event space and multi-brand flagship TGY is designed to change over time, offering guests a different experience from visit to visit. Beijing-based studio Ramoprimo developed its 600-m² interior, which integrates a curated boutique and flexible event hub and gallery where guest designers can showcase new collections, with a café, beauty centre and flower shop.

Tasked with creating a surprising and eye-catching yet classical and cosy design, the team found inspiration for the fluid space in the concept of movement, with a layout characterised by the popping-up of various elements along customers' circulation path.

In the café area, a map of Shenyang installed on lenticular panels changes colour according to the movements of viewers. From here, an arcade of boldface white arches links the café and retail area at opposite ends of the store, inviting customers to venture to the different functional areas.

Curved steel walls resembling swatches of draped textile make up a rotating exhibition room at the entrance of the retail space and a display wall towards the centre. The latter harbours the fitting rooms and storage. Metal serves as the primary material throughout because it offers simultaneously a neutral and dynamic background, reflecting the shapes and colours of garments and changing design elements.

Left Oversized ceramic tiles line the floor. These have a satin metallic finish and are outlined with a glossy steel profile, which reflects the pattern of the ceiling lighting.

Right An arched promenade links the retail floor and café, and serves as a runway, as needed.

Diagrams Two curved steel structures are the key visual and functional elements of the retail floor. One makes up the temporary exhibition room, while the other serves as a display wall which embraces the fitting rooms and storage area.

Metallic surfaces offer, simultaneously, a neutral and dynamic background

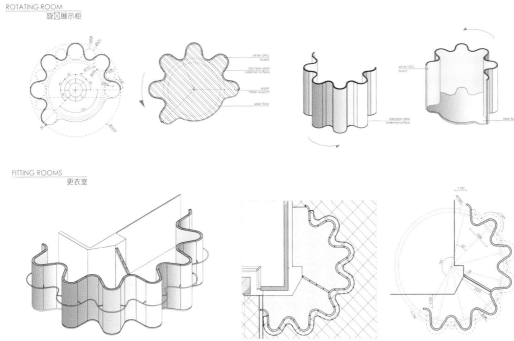

ROTATING ROOM
旋区展示柜

FITTING ROOMS
更衣室

Right In the café, the colours of a wall-size map of Shenyang mounted to lenticular panels shift according to the viewers' movements.

Plan The 600-m² multifunctional space accommodates fashion events for 80 to 100 people.

THE ANIMAL BACKBONE

With a single sculptural gesture, FUN UNIT DESIGN creates a highly functional, flexible space rooted in memory and narrative

Left Built in a former slaughterhouse, this luminous 'experience space' educates the public about animals and how to care for them through art shows, outreach and retail.

Above Prefabricated in under a month at several factories, the stainless steel 'backbone' serves multiple functions and defines the space in a deceptively simple way.

SHANGHAI – The tagline for Fun Unit Design's client, Pidan, is 'Live Better with Pets'. This 100-m² educational animal rights 'experience space' is tucked into a sprawling and sinuous Brutalist building. Its glazed storefront glows like a beacon and appears to float beneath and, improbably, to support the monumental weight of the concrete architecture surrounding it. Designed by Balfour in 1933, the building was once the site of the largest slaughterhouse in the Far East. Co-opting this vast killing field, Pidan memorialises the slaughter and teaches people to care for animals, hosting everything from educational programmes about the euthanisation of abandoned strays, to art exhibitions and feedings that let the public interact with animals.

The sculptural space resembles a giant animal emerging from the earth. Its partly exposed spine forms walls and openings, defines circulation, and displays artwork and products, clarifying the space's multifunctional layout and defining flexible and diverse interior structures. With its generous doorways and floor-level 'mouse holes', the space works at two scales, that of both human and animal guests. Made from stainless steel, the 'backbone' is perforated with 480,000 holes, a memorial to, and abstract story about, the countless loss of life on the site long ago.

Shi Zheng

Left A single design element forms doors, walls, alcoves and 'mouse holes', as well as quasi-intimate pockets.

Above The 480,000 perforations in the steel backbone honour the countless animal lives lost in the former slaughter-house.

Plan A series of abutting circular zones, the backbone manages to function at the scale of both the human and the animal.

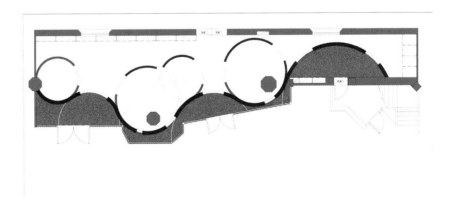

With its generous doorways and floor-level 'mouse holes', the space works at two scales, that of both human and animal guests

Above The space – translucent, smooth, reflective, welcoming – stands in counter-point to the monumental aloofness of the building, designed in 1933 by Balfours.

UNI_JOY

ANYSCALE reimagines
the traditional mall, turning
interstitial space into the
main attraction

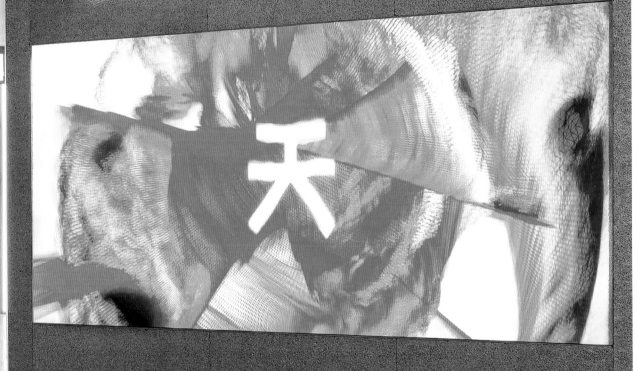

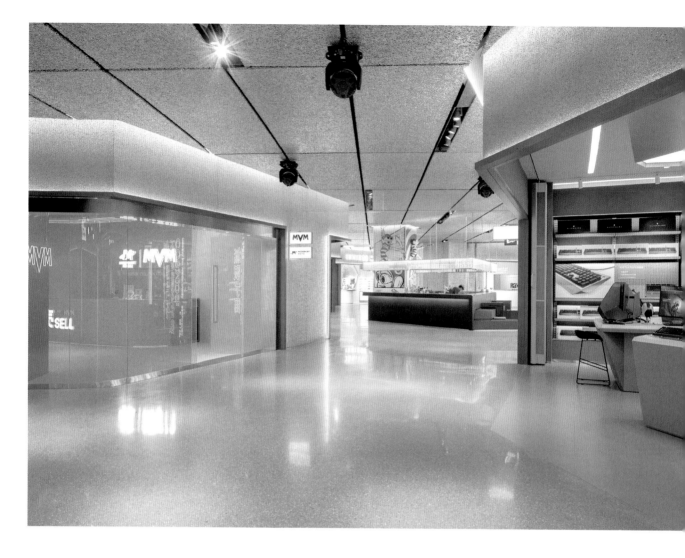

BEIJING – On the fourth floor of the Joy City shopping mall, a 1800-m² shop-in-shop space for multiple young local brands, dubbed Uni_Joy, recognises the role of shoppers' sense of discovery and overall experience in increasing sales and deepening brand loyalty. Commissioned by the mall, Anyscale drafted an irregular plan that groups individual stores around a lively party space.

To emphasise the party theme, allusions to the dance club environment include elements like a bar, DJ table and violet LED lighting displays – all atypical in a mall setting. Design lead Karin Hepp also wanted to make customers feel as if they were floating in outer space, so the team used air-blown aluminium foam (the same light but robust material used in aircraft fuselage) to clad most surfaces. Garment displays and artworks suspended from the ceiling add to the sense of weightlessness.

The choice of one overarching colour in two leading materials – the ceiling and walls' aforementioned grey aluminium foam and grey terrazzo flooring – invokes a glossy luxury. More importantly, it provides a neutral environment in which to frame each colourful storefront, guiding the gaze of shoppers. In this simultaneously sleek and playful, neutral and vibrant environment, the area between the stores becomes the primary driver of consumer's curiosity.

Previous Spread One colour, two materials: Grey terrazzo flooring with walls and ceilings clad in grey aluminium foam provide a neutral frame for the vivid storefronts.

Left Combining shop-in-shop brand space with a lively party and event area, Uni_Joy attracts customers thanks to a unique shopping experience.

Right and Below The design team fitted a pop-up shop next to the event area, adding to the appeal of limited-time offer purchases.

Xia Zhi

The choice of one overarching colour in two leading materials provides a neutral environment in which to frame each colourful storefront

Left Colourful LED screens stand out from the neutral background, attracting attention to specific focal points, like the DJ table.

Above Event programmes and artistic video installations created by one of the vendors, the MVM design label, animate the space.

Plan Individual stores are wrapped around an event and party space in a somewhat irregular plan, which invites exploration and discovery.

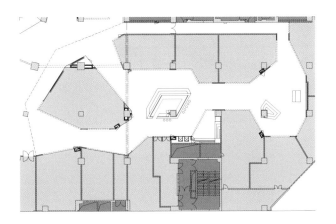

Left ZiinLife Café is one of the brand's stores designed by Supercloud in four years.

Above Founded in 2015, ZiinLife has been well-received by young Chinese consumers, but needed to extend its online retail, offline.

ZIINLIFE CAFÉ

SUPERCLOUD draws inspiration from theatre sets to create an engaging spatial narrative

SHANGHAI – The second of several stores Supercloud Studio designed for ascendant Chinese housewares brand ZiinLife matches its tagline: 'Life is full of beautiful surprises'. It sits in a free-standing, three-storey former office building whose grey granite façade used to blend in with surrounding buildings. Supercloud completely redesigned the façade, cladding it with a skin of perforated folding metal panels in order to give the dark, heavy, time-worn structure a lighter, fresher look. The design team painted the ground floor's façade matte black, added a white powder-coated aluminium parapet and layered the windows with rainbow film. The perforated panels and film filter light that flows in and out of the building, embroidering the street and store with patterns and hue.

Inside, the 560-m² store serves multiple functions – furniture showroom, café, library and a space for finding inspiration –, and has rapidly become a popular gathering place for young people. The designers envisioned the journey through the interiors as a theatrical experience in three scenes, or stations – 'Pink Elephant', 'Timber Box' and '2017' – each occupying one floor. These distinctive scenographies tempt visitors to explore and allow them to make discoveries at almost every turn.

Left 'Pink Elephant' is constructed from pink metal mesh over a steel frame.

Above Like the other two stations or 'scenes', the '2017' installation of suspended white metal mesh partitions fills an entire floor.

Diagrams Each of the store's three scenes, or stations, occupies one floor.

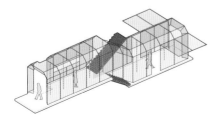  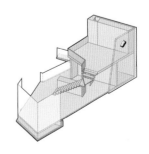

Left 'Timber Box', dressed entirely in particle board, was inspired by a one-bedroom loft apartment.

Right Top In ZiinLife's Joy City store, individual furniture showcases populate an M C Escher-like space of cellular but porous vignettes that determine how shoppers navigate the space.

Right Bottom At ZiinLife Livat centre, a series of concentric circles makes each display of products stand out whilst generating an unconventional, but intriguing, circulation path through the space.

Distinct scenographies tempt visitors to explore and allow them to make discoveries at every turn

KEY TAKEAWAYS

With the entrenchment of our lives online, physical stores have evolved from sales spaces into social milieux and increasingly complex expressions of lifestyle.

For many retailers, in-store sales are no longer the driver of physical retail. Instead, they see shopping as an experience that customers hold on to – and share.

As China's retail landscape changes, an appetite for multifaceted, lifestyle-focused venues which incorporate online shopping with offline showcases becomes apparent. These hybrid spaces are designed to be flexible, ever-changing, one-stop destinations for fashion, experience, education and wellness.

But as interdisciplinary and cross-brand experiences become mainstream, designers must continuously reinvent the typology. For example, by not only combining multiple businesses in one location, but making different retail formats complementary.

Wow

Factor

Boosting brand engagement through surprising, innovative and oftentimes transient experiences.

As competition for consumers' attention (and spending power) increases, brands are working with designers to develop ever more innovative, surprising and transitional in-store experiences. It becomes a vicious cycle – the more out-of-the-box brick-and-mortar stores become, the higher consumers' expectations are – and that's great news for the industry: the bar of quality retail design is set higher and higher. This chapter collects key examples of projects whose playful – and sometimes starkly simple – layouts embrace surprise and encourage discovery and exploration.

.JPG COFFEE

GEOMDESIGN uses a minimal, but impactful façade to help a kiosk stand out in a crowded business district

GUANGZHOU – Tasked with creating an impactful design for a kiosk in Zhujiang New Town's central business district, local studio GeomDesign reverted to a simple, natural material: red brick. At only 38-m², .jpg coffee caters to the area's fast-paced lifestyle, serving drinks and burgers out of a pair of black aluminium and stainless steel openings.

The designers' first challenge was that the style of the take-out-only eatery needed to be completely different from its surroundings. The chosen natural material – sintered red brick – makes the diminutive space stand out against the sterile backdrop of the district's towering glazed buildings. Thanks to the bricks' colour, texture and the position in which they are lain, this solution isn't only eco-friendly, but a highly powerful, if subdued, design gesture.

By creating a bevelled frame around the black openings, the design attracts focus to the coffee and food production processes inside. What is more, the absence of logos and branded information ensure that the pure architectural storefront draws customers' attention to the products, rather than a brand image.

1. Outlet 2. Single station 3. Operator 4. Cup rack

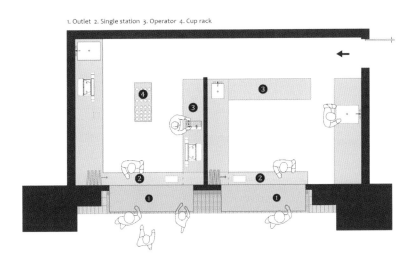

Previous Spread This coffee and burger kiosk is fronted with sintered brick made from natural clay, argil, shale and other primary eco-friendly minerals that, after the life of the building, can be crushed and recycled.

Left The architects worked closely with the builders to create the exterior wall, with its two eye-socket-like bevels around the black metal service windows and no visible mortar seams.

Plan Inside, the small space is split into two areas, one for the baristas and another for the confection of hamburgers.

Foregoing logos, the pure architectural storefront draws attention to the products, rather than a brand image

HOLILAND

DAS LAB reinterprets a bakery as an experimental lab and concept store

SHANGHAI – For a 80-m² bakery and pastry concept shop, experimental design studio Das Lab abstracted elements from the post-industrial era to create an environment that celebrates mechanical aesthetics and food industry innovation. The cold inertness and homogeneity of the chosen materials – sandblasted stainless steel with carefully integrated lighting, foamed aluminium, Bestmo terrazzo floors, volcanic stone – contrast with the organic warmth and colourful profusion of the baked goods on display.

The designers envisioned the space as a factory made up of systems, where the products displayed – made with precision and control – are treated like industrial objects. Mechanical elements allude to the rapid advance of standardisation and automation technologies. For example, an overhead conveyor belt with radiused corners and an endlessly rotating spherical flour container, presented abstractly, can be adapted as display surfaces.

Different materials are stitched, overlapped and extended to offer the most direct way to read the space. Materials in a grey tone, like the foamed aluminium and stainless steel, glow under panels of light film stretched across the ceiling. The low colour saturation of the materials ensures that the mechanical devices emphasise the products, while still playing the protagonists of the space, as well. Overall, the design wraps visitors in an experimental lab, allowing them to experience the complexity of the mechanised world and to connect with the brand in multiple ways.

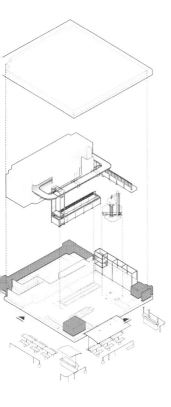

Previous Spread This fresh interpretation of the bakery mixes the new technologies and increasing creativity being brought to bear in the food industry and the disciplines orbiting it.

Left The mechanical components of the interior, like the overhead conveyor belt, nod to the galloping development of standardisation and automation.

Right Materials in a grey tone, like foamed aluminium and stainless steel, glow under panels of light film stretched across the ceiling.

Next Spread The project tapped elements from the post-industrial age to create an interior featuring machine aesthetics as counterpoint to the creative confections they showcase.

Diagram An outdoor seating area flanks the corner store and follows the same lab-like aesthetic of the interiors.

Shao Feng

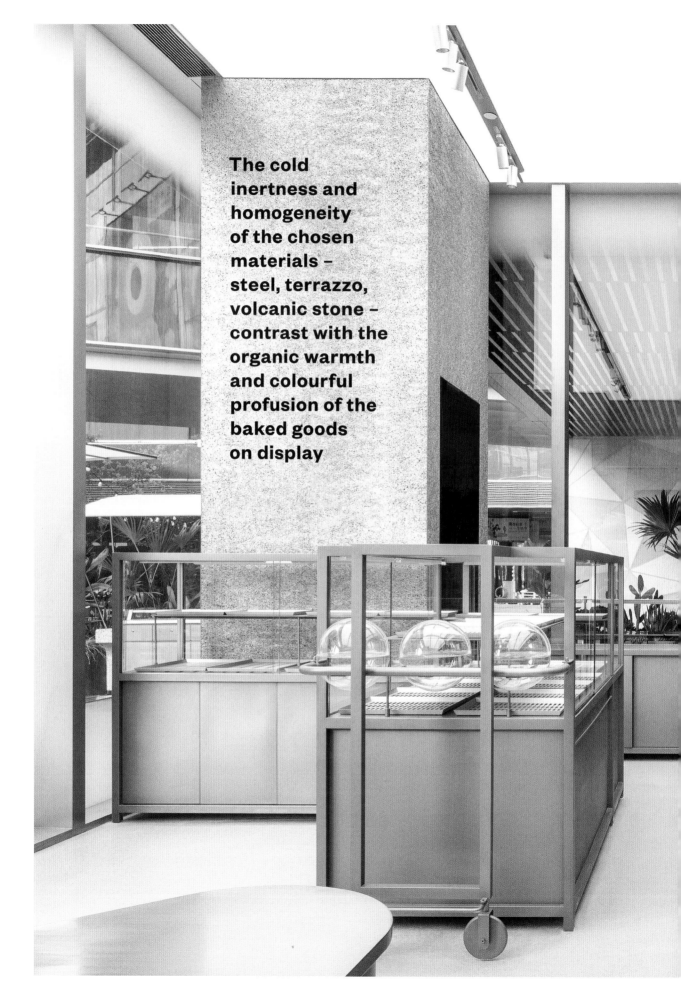

The cold inertness and homogeneity of the chosen materials – steel, terrazzo, volcanic stone – contrast with the organic warmth and colourful profusion of the baked goods on display

COORDINATION ASIA's curated retail experience for Nike explores the process of innovation through changing installations

Charlie Xia

Left At the heart of Coordination Asia's installation for the launch of Noise Cancelling Pack is a sculptural work comprising 120 speakers which channel street-sourced sounds to the interior, quite literally bringing the outside in.

Above The installation's audio output is tracked on an adjacent LED screen wall by way of a precise graph, with the linear motif repeated throughout the space.

SHANGHAI – In this experimental and experience-driven flagship store, regularly changing installations by local studio Coordination Asia depict moments in the history of Nike's celebrated design innovation. The tightly curated shopping experience offers visitors a peek behind the scenes into examples of the brand's industry-changing shifts in areas ranging from research to production.

The studio creates immersive thematic vignettes for the collections presented in the flagship. But in lieu of typical merchandising methods – constructing a stage on which the products play the brand's protagonists – the designers turn the retail floor into a narrative environment made-to-measure for Chinese consumers. The technical details and technology behind the creation of each product displayed are transformed into story-telling installations that not only allow consumers to understand the products from a technical perspective, but to more actively engage with the creative process.

Every few weeks, as featured collections change, the theme – along with the entire space – changes too. Each 'make-over' of the black box interiors represents a fresh iteration of the innovation concept rendered as a part-industrial and part-scientific laboratory environment. By shining a light on the 'backstage' of product design and manufacturing, the installations go well beyond two-dimensional logos and three-dimensional brand identities to provide a 360-degree retail experience.

Above For the launch of the Air19 collection, the designers created an experimental lab-like environment. One of the interactive installations recreates the production process where air is injected into the sole via exposed tubes connected to an inflated plastic bubble.

Right Acrylic, plastic, steel machinery parts and exposed tubes are used to formulate a lab-like space where people are encouraged to explore and experiment.

VAPORWEAVE

CARBON-FIBER LAUNCHPAD

ZOOMX

H LINE, AND WE WANT TO CONTINUE
PORFLY DESIGN, ALWAYS LOOKING TO
ADVANTAGE ON RACE DAY
通过不断优化VAPORFLY跑鞋的设计,
突破

NIKE   OR   NEXT%
OUR   S   ER   3知的快

NIKE ZOOMX
VAPORFLY NEXT

NIKE AIR ZOOM PEGASUS 36

NIKE ZOOM PEGASUS TURBO 2

NIKE ZOOM FLY 3

NIKE ZOOMX VAPORFLY NEXT

The installations go well beyond two-dimensional logos and three-dimensional brand identities to provide a 360-degree retail experience

Previous spread A striking floor-to-ceiling digital ticker installation for Nike's Fast Pack 2019 collection comprises constantly flashing LED lights on four black metal frames, capturing customers' attention at the entrance and setting the mood for the entire retail experience.

Above At the centre of the installation, stands made of digital tickers display the collection.

Right Top Nike's House of Innovation concept is an experimental flagship where the science museum-like interior changes frequently according to the themes of a collection.

Right Bottom The installations visualise some of the brand's watershed innovations from its creative processes to its production techniques and technology.

IN THE PARK

KOOO ARCHITECTS studies the playground to bring surprise, engagement and irregularity to a multi-brand store

Left A hint of greenery floods the park-like interior from a window.

Above In the Park is a multi-brand concept shop that borrows the joyful irregular organisation of a playground and eschews the more rigid arrangement of furniture in clothing shops.

Below Like a park, the shop has a floor made with concrete 'cobblestones'.

Right The interior slightly abstracts playground furniture and scatters it throughout as seating or display, making the shop engagingly discoverable.

SHANGHAI – Hoping to invite a wider demographic of shoppers, Kooo Architects drew inspiration from the public nature of parks to design a boutique for multi-brand Chinese retailer ZucZug. The architects imagined the 254-m² concept store as a free and relaxed environment for patrons of any and all ages, a playground that they based on studies of the organisation of amusement parks and play areas.

The team placed display shelves against the walls vertically as a simple and efficient way to showcase products, but most of the furnishings and entertainment in an amusement park are arranged in a variety of irregular positions in order to stoke the enthusiasm of children. This is how the designers organised unorthodox displays of playground-like furniture, including a variety of see-saws and spring-loaded surfaces. Instead of placing the product at a standard height where it is easy for most customers to touch it, they placed displays at various heights, making many items and details feel discoverable. The design team embraced the notion of creating an irregularly ordered retail space in order to stimulate the senses and entertain shoppers of all stripes.

XU STUDIO's lab-inspired design gives consumers an immediate, entertaining experience of both brand and product

Peter Zhang

SHANGHAI – At just 26-m², a mobile pop-up built out of a shipping container represents a prestige beauty and skincare label's first foray into physical retail. Local designers XU Studio helped Junping transition from an online to offline presence by repurposing a 12-m-wide by 2.8-m-high container to bring the brand directly to its target audience at universities and shopping centres across the country.

A façade made up of transparent acrylic tubes and punctuated by linear luminaires at irregular intervals blurs the flow of movement in the interior and sets the stage for the pop-up. Inside, in order to demonstrate both the future-forward character and the more mystical aspects of beauty products, the design team created a laboratory environment through the use of bold lighting and associated materials like stainless steel, white surfaces, beakers and test tubes.

Beneath a luminous light film that simulates a skylight, products are displayed along a stainless steel wall illuminated with neon lights. A key feature of the store, a 3.7-m-long lab counter at the entrance encourages the taking and sharing of selfies, and is equipped with three 'magic' mirrors, which analyse visitors' skin, allowing them to detect possible issues and to receive personalised and customisable product recommendations.

A key feature of the lab environment, 'magic' mirrors analyse visitors' skin and provide personalised and customisable product recommendations

PEU À PEU BY JNBY

SÒ STUDIO turns the tropes of physical training into a kinetic sportswear boutique

HANGZHOU – For women's sportswear brand Peu à Peu's retail space, Shanghai-based design practice Sò Studio was inspired in part by the 'eternally optimistic' reflective sculptures in artist Jeff Koons' Celebration series, and in part by the rudimentary mechanics of athletic activity.

Along the perimeter of the 70-m² room, the designers used straps to bind sponge foam, mylar matts and volleyballs to structural columns, creating a collage of high-contrast materials. Among these and against a minimal background of light grey floor, walls and ceiling, an elaborate stainless steel installation dominates the room.

The apparatus runs through the room like an oversize pinball machine, its tracks holding large metal spheres, chin-up bar-like garment racks and surfaces resembling simplified weightlifting machinery. The installation doubles as a detachable garment display system and a means to organise the space into different zones. It also resembles a kinetic Rube Goldberg machine: With a piston-like up-and-down motion, a robot arm drives the movement of the metal spheres along the steel track, allowing the specular reflection of the balls to mirror changes in the surrounding environment at rest and in motion. The robot arm also stamps down periodically on a potato chip bag, repeating a whimsical process in which calories are, quite literally, crushed.

Left Taking the form of objects like weight machines or chin-up bars, the installation also serves as a display system.

Above Straps bind various sports-related objects together – foam matt, mylar cushion, volleyballs – against columns at the room's edges.

Next Spread An otherwise simple room contains an intricate stainless steel installation that dominates this women's sportswear boutique.

An elaborate stainless steel installation dominates the room, serving both as display system and space organiser

GENTLE MONSTER uses unexpected narratives to redefine customers' interaction with a luxury emporium

BEIJING – Looking to redefine the way a department store interacts with customers, Gentle Monster began the design process for luxury mall SKP-S by pondering on humanity's future: What will it be like? Between technological development and human evolution, what will be missed, valued and worth fighting for? A forward and backward-looking meditation on the nature of the present, the future and ourselves, the ensuing project, titled 'Future Analogue', presents narratives filled with nostalgia from the perspective of the future.

On the first floor, instead of the typical department store counters of jewellery, watches or luxury fragrances, shoppers encounter a herd of robotic sheep created by Gentle Monster's own robotics LAB to tell a story: Caught somewhere between human instinct and control by AI, a future generation longs for the past and, in response, creates the robotic herd in an effort to recall an analogue era. Elsewhere, the tunnel-like corridors of a spaceship suggest passageways to an unknown place where visitors find artefacts of little value now, but that people of the future will have found emotionally meaningful. In another mise-en-scène, an old man converses with an AI who looks almost identical to him.

The vignettes are unexpected and thought-provoking. Shoppers may wonder: Is this a mall, or a museum? Is this the future, or is it now? 'In the midst of such a mixture of future and past, new and analogue, shock and admiration,' the designers explain, 'we wanted customers to free themselves of what they expect and what they are used to.'

Previous Spread Gentle Monster's design team turned this 5570-m² luxury department store into a new retail experience for millennials and those always searching for something new.

Left and Below On the first floor, instead of cosmetics counters, Gentle Monster used its own robotics technology to create a herd of sheep as representative of what we may long for in the future.

Gentle Monster

Previous Spread In Gentle Monster's own space in SKP-S, classical sculptures ruminate on what people of the future will remember and value from the past.

Left Gentle Monster not only designed the interiors, but curated brands that retail here, gaining each label's permission to tell their brand story in a fresh way, consonant with the narratives of SKP-S.

Right The varied vignettes are part of a narrative that imagines future humans migrating to Mars, a trope common to many depictions of the future, where their minds would be controlled by AI.

A meditation on the nature of the present, the future and ourselves, the project presents narratives filled with nostalgia from the perspective of the future

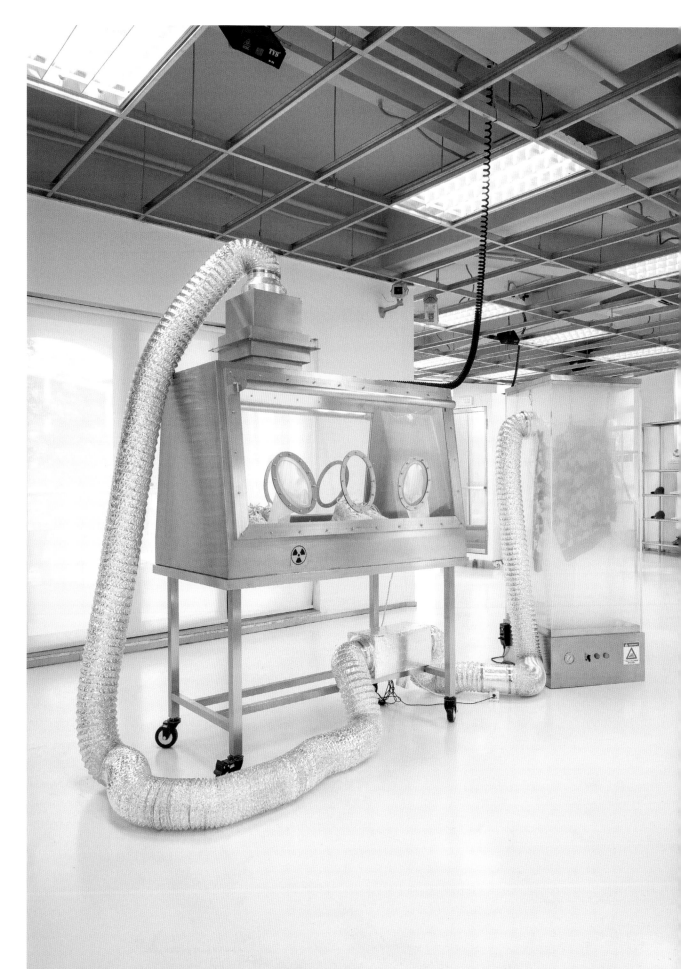

XIANXIANG DESIGN
re-imagines traditional retail space through the lens of street culture

Left The store's first art installation, 'power extraction', displays new products in a metal shell under warm yellow light. Energy extraction is represented by pipes which release smoke into the transparent box beside it.

Above The easily reconfigurable open space features mobile fitting rooms and surfaces that can transform from cash till to DJ booth on a whim.

HANGZHOU – Over the years and around the globe, street culture has become a high-profile and high-profit niche within the fashion industry. This cultural and commercial development has demanded a profound shift in retailing methods away from fashion's aloof, exclusive and explicitly commercial posture toward a creative remix of daily life that resonates more immediately with younger consumers. The Mix Land store sells a curated collection of streetwear brands, but also serves as a destination where those involved with, or interested in, street culture can come together.

XianXiang Design applied 'street thinking' to the interior design, creating interactive experiences in the form of art installations that immediately engage customers. The team envisioned the store as a laboratory, an apt analogy for the embrace of experimentation, perennial change and creative risk-taking that takes place on the street.

The 360-m² space features a shelf display system, mirrors, space accessories and art installations made from metallic materials. Taken together, the three installations – demonstrating the processes of energy extraction, condensation and decomposition – offer visitors an environment in which senses beyond the sight are activated. Through a combination of vision, sound and touch, the design provides an immersive, interactive experience of not just the store and its products, but the brand, as well.

Left White walls and floors create a pure and aseptic environment like that of a lab. This backdrop also serves to increase the contrast with other colours and patterns introduced into the space – like the iridescent film covering the office doors – that share the vivid, neon hues of chemical reactions and street art.

Right The installations and display furnishings – like trainer displays, which resemble sterilisation cabinets – are made from metallic materials like stainless steel and mylar, and take cues from lab equipment.

Next Spread The third installation, 'operation desk', simulates the process of decomposition. Be it the decomposition of matter in a lab, or the deconstruction of streetwear design, the designers hope to highlight the process of removing the superficial and finding new form.

Wang Minjie

Through a combination of vision, sound and touch, the design provides an immersive, interactive experience of the brand

THE SHOUTER

KOSTAS CHATZIGIANNIS ARCHITECTURE explores the boundaries between functionality and art to engage a brand's millennial clientele

SHANGHAI - Selling quirky, playful, limited-edition products, The Shouter is a spin-off from an established retailer in response to growing demand from a younger emancipated Chinese clientele for self-expressive living space – and a surprising retail experience.

On the street façade, this 250-m² multi-brand furniture and home accessories showroom, designed by local firm Kostas Chatzigiannis Architecture, features sleek geometric window openings. Contrastingly, on the interior mall façade and inside the store, massive 35-cm-thick concrete walls seem to have been blasted open by brute force – crumbling edges and cracks abound – to create doorways and clear sightlines. The shop is a study in smooth, refined and flawless versus rugged, raw, and broken. It blends 'almost child-like' spaces with luxury, a contrast studio founder Kostas Chatzigiannis describes as a 'game of contradictions'.

Visitors circulate through entry and exit points, sometimes 'confronted' by large glass cabinets blocking their way. Product displays are found in the centre of the room, recalling forms characteristic of the 1980s Memphis Group movement. LED light structures frame the most important pieces, featuring terrazzo tiles accented with glass marbles and colourful resin boards that complete the material palette. 'As home decoration aspirations in China change constantly, this store does not attempt to define them,' Chatzigiannis says. 'Rather it participates, in an anecdotal way, in the accidental game that creates them.'

The store blends 'almost child-like' spaces with luxury, a contrast the designer describes as a 'game of contradictions'

Previous Spread This furniture and home accessories store approaches the line between functional interior design and art to address the more expressive aspirations of a young Chinese clientele.

Left Custom LED light strips line the edges of bespoke display podiums under an exposed ceiling.

Above Deliberately punching through concrete walls opens sightlines and creates passages leading from one part of the store into others, contrasting with the sleek products and sharp display surfaces.

Right The 'broken' interior walls find their counterpoint in precise, glossy, geometric window openings found on the store's street façade.

Derryck Menere

WHATEVER EYEWEAR

ROOMOO turns a sculptural
kinetic installation into
a store, and vice versa

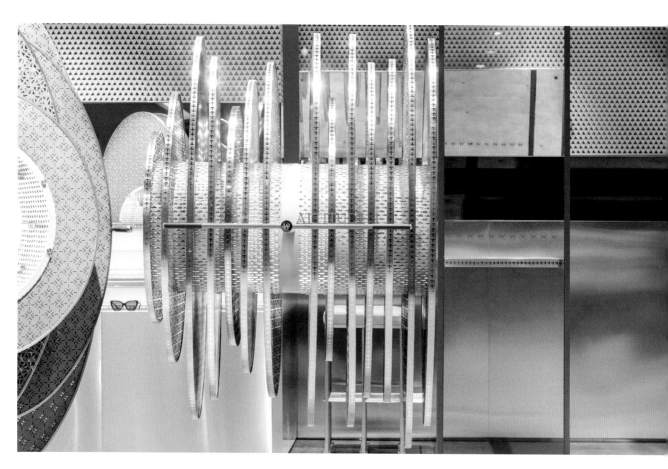

SHANGHAI – Tasked with designing a store for fashion sunglasses brand Whatever Eyewear, RooMoo produced a large pair of movable devices that serve as product display while creating a means of interaction that broadens the customer's experience of the eyewear, sales staff, shop and brand.

Making up the store's primary display, the kinetic structures were inspired by the details of the brand's logo and the character of the products, themselves. For each structure, perforated circles of various sizes are assembled on a central tube, forming a rotating installation that represents the visual image made by the sound vibrations when the words 'whatever' and 'attitude' are vocalised. The circles feature a cut-out arrow pattern and the central tubes a cut-out bullet pattern that, together, form a semi-transparent and relatively lightweight assemblage. The use of aluminium plates allowed the designers to achieve the required detail while reducing the overall weight of the structure.

Product details are easier to view from different angles thanks to lighting set strategically into the central tube and the three-layer transparent acrylic display shelves. The overall shape is divided into upper and lower sections by a central handle, which also takes its cues from the brand's logo. The rotating sculptures can also serve the various needs of scene display because they are suspended via fixed rotational bearings in the ceiling. Ultimately, the sculptural installation provides a shopping adventure for customers, thus facilitating fresh interaction between brand, staff, product and consumer.

Previous Spread The designers considered the 45-m² space as a three-dimensional grid, with all ceiling, floor and wall claddings designed to a standard size, prefabricated and assembled on-site.

Left Top The primary, movable display is a visual representation of the sound-waves made by the words 'whatever' and 'attitude' when spoken.

Left Bottom RooMoo helped develop the brand's image through the shop's spatial details.

Below The store's walls, clad in stainless steel perforated plates, feature the brand's signature colours, grey and red.

Xiaoyun

ATELIER ARCHMIXING and SUPERCLOUD bring together interior design and media art to extend customer experience beyond physical boundaries

SHANGHAI – Yitiao.tv, a video-focused content producer and e-commerce start-up, entered brick-and-mortar retail with a bang when it opened three offline stores totalling nearly 1000-m², along with a modular pop-up shop. The environments, by Atelier Archmixing and Supercloud Studio, represent an intersection of interior architecture and micro-architecture with media art in order to extend guests' perception beyond the merely physical.

Just as the goods on the online platform of Yitiao.tv are refreshed daily, so are the goods sold offline. To support this unusually rapid rotation of goods and décor offline, the designers created both large props as part of the more scenographic zones, and smaller, more flexible displays to facilitate the quickest changes.

To increase traffic and the capacity of the double-height loft space in the Xinzhuang Store (pictured here), the design teams created six 'devices'. For example, 'Yidatiao' is an architectural installation made from lightweight flat steel that combines stairs, display shelves and multimedia content on video screens of varying dimensions that will draw visitors to the upper floor. Likewise, video screens and canopies above the coffee bar attract shoppers to that social area. The designers also sculpted two passages – a series of pink arches forming a small corridor and a white hut-shaped opening – that connect to isolated rooms on the upper floor. These are seen by denizens of the Internet as 'rabbit holes' – portals into alternate worlds –, and have become a destination for savvy netizens.

Previous Spread Yitiao.tv took its e-commerce business offline when its founder decided that physical retail could enrich its online retail at relatively small expense.

Below Screens of various dimensions, featuring lifestyle content, are integrated throughout much of the store, like in the cashier area.

Right The designers created larger furnishings and props to define the space, while smaller props facilitate rapid changes.

Wu Qingshan

Left This portal is one of two passages linking discrete rooms on the upper floor, both of which are recognised by savvy netizens as metaphorical 'rabbit holes'.

Above The designers created larger furnishings and props to define the space, but opted for small props as a more flexible way to facilitate rapid changes.

The design supports an unusually rapid rotation of goods and décor

KEY TAKEAWAYS

Diverging from the traditional conviction that display must be regular and orderly to be effective, stores should instead embrace layouts that encourage exploration and discovery.

Typical department stores bombard shoppers with glaring lights and too much choice, instead of inspiration and wonder. By creating spaces that ask customers to explore and imagine, designers can improve engagement.

To win the loyalty of repeat customers, designers must find ways to accommodate quick changes of displays, experience and content in both large and small scales, promoting a continuous sense of curiosity.

Creating a spatial balance between playfulness and sophistication can attract an audience from baby boomers to Gen Z.

But even when it comes to creating surprise, sometimes less is more. When designing in a crowded, artificial environment, the pure and the organic often make the biggest impact.

Narr
Sp

ating
nce

Boosting brand engagement through compelling spatial narratives which guide the customer's journey.

One of the most sweeping – and perhaps most counter-intuitive – consequences of the rise of e-commerce has been to witness product display in brick-and-mortar stores take a backseat to a space's capacity to enrich customer experience. By developing compelling spatial narratives which guide customers' journeys, designers and retailers are able to boost brand engagement, both in-store and out. From the integration of digital media to the interpretation of the fitting room as a theatre stage, this chapter gathers inspiring examples of what the storytelling model for physical retail can look like.

BRLOOTE

GREATER DOG ARCHITECTS
translates Kazimir Malevich's iconic Black Square into a three-dimensional white canvas

Left For a purist fashion brand entering the Chinese market, Greater Dog reinterpreted a painting into a three- dimensional space.

Above The interior represents the combination of functionality and art.

SHAOXING – Designed by Greater Dog Architects, this 830-m² Chinese flagship for Dutch fashion label Brloote represents the translation of a two-dimensional painting into a three-dimensional retail space. Kazimir Malevich, a strong, long-time influence on Iraqi-British architect Zaha Hadid, was a Russian Suprematist artist and theorist. His famous Black Square (circa 1913), which the artist described as reducing everything to the zero of form, is symbolic of a turning point in the art world. The painting reminded Greater Dog Architects of its client's trend-eschewing menswear collections, which are largely made up of black, white and grey garments. Indeed, comfort, quality and detail are the main features – the zero of form – of the label's fabric and materials.

In the store then, the architects applied geometric shapes of various dimensions, from lines to solid forms that intersect, overlap and avoid each other. Adhering to the Constructivist notion of multiple viewpoints in space, the team divided the shop into two parts using a thin black line and then began 'trying to stretch, cross, rotate and place the black square on a clean white spatial canvas to form a pure physical structure.'

The result is an enticing interior, which changes, extends and grows with the customers' imagination and the brand's interpretation of its function.

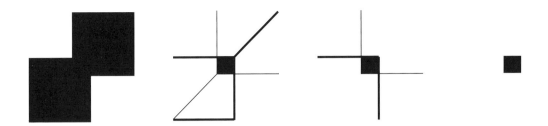

The interior changes and grows with the customers' imagination and the brand's interpretation of its function

Left Product displays are also derived from a geometric conception of space.

Right and Sketch The designers started by trying to manipulate a black square on a clean white spatial canvas to create the structure of the store. The illustrations represent steps one, three, seven and ten of this manipulation.

Rachel Wu & Red Hu

BY JOVE

A multifunctional flower shop by MUR MUR LAB is designed like a poem

Arttteeezy

HANGZHOU – A versatile 200-m² flower shop, By Jove serves several functions: a café, housewares shop and floral design learning space. For all its uses, however, it is made of few, simple, materials: white terrazzo, gauze curtain, clear acrylic – and poetry. Mur Mur Lab partners, Xia Murong and Li Zhi, wrote 12 short poems for the client, imagining each scenario the space might contain, while putting aside practical thoughts of structure. A key starting point for the design, the poems considered light, shadow and flowers before space. As the designers put it, '[In By Jove], the summation of every part is greater than the whole.'

Steeped in imagination and mood, the store's dramatic narrative begins outside. The storefront interrupts a grey city street with a field of white and blue. Inside, white surfaces serve as the background for colourful flowers and products. Whites of different textures and translucencies (gauze, cement, terrazzo, acrylic, glass) are spread out along a slightly curved path. These subtly different whites become vibrant when suffused with natural light, and are interrupted by big cobalt blue 'pauses'. When the blue gathers into a tunnel leading up a spiral staircase, visitors seem to leave light behind, however, at the darkest point, they re-emerge into a 'starry' night sky, thanks to dream-like, starry lighting embedded in the ceiling.

雨是一种漂亮的动物

E.E.卡明斯

The Rain is a Handsome Animal

E.E. Cummings

Samoon

Samoon

A key starting point for the design, Mur Mur Lab's poems considered light, shadow and flowers before space

DONGQI ARCHITECTS
transforms a century-old
building into a retail space
with two contrasting interiors

Qingshan Wu

Left and Above Glimpses of the
old/new dichotomy can be seen in the
building's façade, as door and windows are
framed in stainless steel, contrasting with
the old bricks.

Left A row of existing columns in the centre of the building posed a potential challenge, but the team saw it as an advantage and added two extra rows of pillars, creating an umbrella-shaped system that clarifies the circulation and brings drama to the space.

Right Opposing walls are surfaced in mirror-finish stainless steel and concrete, a visual trick to widen the space and multiply the columns.

Next Spread The store's back space – built with anodic aluminium oxide, stainless steel, carbon fibre and terrazzo – is designed to be in complete juxtaposition with the front.

SHANGHAI – To design the first Chinese flagship for street fashion label Concept, dongqi Architects refurbished a century-old heritage building, preserving the original Shikumen architectural elements at the front of the store, and cladding the rear with contemporary metallic finishes. These contrasting approaches allowed the team to create two distinct interiors in the 290-m² shop, so that it is has the capacity for hosting diverse cultural – not just commercial – content. This visual contrast also reflects the operational need to reconcile dual functions: day-to-day sales and the release of limited-edition sneakers.

'We retained the "old" at the entry area to offer a cosy ambiance, ideal for reception, product shows and events,' the designers explain.

While at the back of the store, materials like anodic aluminium oxide, stainless steel, metal textiles and carbon fibre provide a futuristic setting for sales. Here, two rows of pillars were added, one at each side of an existing central row, creating an umbrella-shaped cladding system that supports independent product display areas.

Shutter-like slats were created using an algorithm that modified their angles, depending on height. This aesthetic element – anchored by stainless-steel joints designed, prototyped and produced for the brand – serves as display and conceals mechanical systems. Each joint features three-axis rotation so as to fix materials firmly to a position, enable custom functions, and create adjustable display racks, fitting room walls, doorknobs and hangers.

The interior's visual contrast reflects the operational need to reconcile dual functions: day-to-day sales and the release of limited-edition sneakers

Above and Left The team opted to retain the original Shikumen elements of the building in the entry area as it offers a warm, sociable ambiance ideal for reception and events, product shows and sneaker releases.

Right Bespoke three-axis steel joints serve as a brand-owned architectural element which can be carried forward in new spaces, as the brand expands in more Chinese cities. Besides supporting the store's defining element – the shutter-like slats –, the joints also support adjustable display racks, the walls of the fitting rooms, doorknobs and hangers.

GEIJOENG CONCEPT STORE

STUDIO 10 brings the fitting room to the centre of customers' experience – and the design concept

SHENZHEN – Glass, stone, acrylic and fabric are common enough in retail interiors, but this 120-m^2 boutique for minimalist womenswear label Geijoeng layers atypical forms of these materials: Channel glass, glass brick, mirror and custom terrazzo render the space airy, bright, deep and textural. Designed by Studio 10 in just over one month, the ethereal-looking interior embodies the brand's commitment to working with the finest materials and craftsmanship and serves as an Instagrammable environment.

Inside, the mirage-like translucence of the channel glass-clad walls finds its counterpart in a floor paved with bespoke greyish-green terrazzo studded with oversize dark green and white marble aggregate. Frosted acrylic rods fixed with metal scaffolding joints and set into green marble podiums of various sizes, make garment display easily adjustable.

Front and centre, the acrylic tube-enclosed fitting room recalls a small stage. In green velour Kvadrat fabric by Raf Simons, the curtain that lines the room gives privacy and builds anticipation when closed; but when open, leaves the shop and fitting room partially visible to one another. This theatrical effect suggests that the wearer of fashion is as much a nexus of creativity as fashion itself: Customers enter the shop as spectators but leave as the protagonists.

Previous Spread At the centre of the store – and the design concept – is the fitting room: What is normally a purely functional space becomes a focal point.

Below and Right The entrance corridor and window display are paved with glass brick backgrounded with the brand's signature greyish-green paint. Here, a semi-reflective glass wall and mirrored drop ceiling generate unexpected compositions and depth.

Chao Zhang

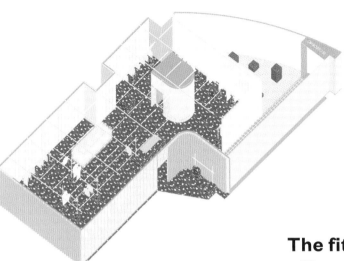

The fitting room's theatrical effect suggests that the wearer of fashion is as much a nexus of creativity as fashion itself

Previous Spread Garment racks are made of frosted acrylic rods fastened with metal scaffolding joints that make them easy to adjust and reconfigure.

Left The interior flooring is paved with custom greyish-green terrazzo embedded with large dark green and white marble aggregate.

Right The acrylic-tube-enclosed fitting room is lined with a theatrical green velour curtain from Raf Simons' collection for Kvadrat.

Diagram The fitting room is placed unconventionally and conspicuously at the centre of the space, creating a theatrical effect.

GLORIA

I IN's far-out statement for a store's entrance is all the introduction the fashion label needs

GUANGZHOU – This 290-m² concept shop was designed to introduce Chinese women's clothing brand Gloria to the world. Japanese studio I IN accomplished this with a strong, atmospheric visual statement visible from the store's entrance in a shopping centre corridor.

The store is composed of three zones. The first – the entry area – introduces customers to the brand identity. Here, a sprawling chandelier made up of many small spherical pendant lights clustered into a hemisphere above a living tree hints at a voyage beneath a starlit sky. A wall display of backlit brand visuals narrates its history and visual DNA, completing the introduction.

The second part of the design is the product display. A horizontal light set into shallow ledges at eye level extends around the walls of the entire space, representing the Earth's horizon and guiding customers deeper into the store. On the upper wall, graphics, painted by Japanese illustrator Chalkboy, depict parts of the world map. Gently arching wooden display bars showcase the clothes within a softened frame, emphasising the feminine sophistication of the space.

Finally, in the VIP room at the rear of the store, lights are scattered at different heights and distances from one other. Here, too, the lighting gives the dim chamber a dream-like atmosphere, as if visitors were, themselves, suspended among the constellations.

Previous Spread A tree grows beneath pendant lighting that outlines the bottom half of a globe, the anchoring element of the space's narrative of a journey around the planet.

Below Glossy mall floors reflect the starry façade of this fashion concept shop, hinting at the unique universe within.

Right A horizontal wall light, symbolising the horizon, leads visitors into the store while upper wall graphics by Chalkboy illustrate a map of the world.

Tomooki Kengaku

253

I IN

In the VIP room, lighting gives the dim chamber a dream-like atmosphere, as if visitors were, themselves, suspended among the constellations

Previous Spread The concave silhouettes of the garment racks offer a feminine frame for the clothing.

Left Irregularly placed globe lights and their reflections make the VIP room appear to float like a starry night sky.

Above Lights hung at different heights from a low drop ceiling help recreate the randomness of the heavens.

SPACEMEN creates a holistic brand experience through the interplay of architecture, nature and smart living technology

Min Chen Xuan and Simon Liu

Previous Spread A 10-m-high atrium and spiral staircase anchor the interiors.

Above On a crowded street, the translucent polycarbonate storefront of the Haier Smart Experience Centre is serene and minimal, becoming a lustrous lantern at night.

Right Small Zen gardens frame views from the bathroom, but also give visitors a moment to pause before entering 'The Smart Home' area.

SHANGHAI – To help consumers understand how the world's first series of 'one-stop' smart home solutions will actually shape their daily lives, home appliances brand Haier tapped local design studio Spacemen to turn its flagship into a domestic idyll that sometimes bears no trace at all of the complex tech that runs behind it.

Spacemen made the Haier Smart Experience Centre a space of calm in a crowded shopping area. Translucent polycarbonate panels turn the façade into a minimalist white box that stands out clearly amidst the busy storefronts nearby. At night, it becomes a glowing lantern. Inside, customers find a 10-m circular atrium and spiral staircase surrounded by four LED-panelled columns playing 360-degree imagery via projectors concealed in the curved walls.

The showroom has three main areas, dubbed 'The Smart Home', 'The Future', and the 'Product Experience Zone'. The design team equipped the first with a living room,

kitchen, bathroom and bedroom in natural oak timber and terrazzo, and fringed with foliage. Each room is kitted out with the latest intelligent appliances, which communicate with each other, enabling a single centralized control, even remotely.

Everywhere, digital screens and projectors fit seamlessly into wall panels and cabinets, activating as customers approach. Guests can also interact with Haier's Smart Home Cloud platform to harvest real-time information about the products, which they can also monitor and control using an app.

The customer journey unfolds into an immersive cinematic experience which highlights the brand's latest technologies in 'The Future', and culminates in the 'Product Experience Zone', where Haier's products are displayed, alongside those of its premium kitchen brand, Casarte.

Left A soft palette of natural oak timber, off white walls and terrazzo define the interior of 'The Smart Home'.

Right Top 'The Future' zone is an immersive, motion-activated, multimedia experience where real and virtual elements, scenography and brand communications demonstrate the latest tech.

Right Bottom The 'Product Experience Zone' displays Haier products alongside those of its premium kitchen brand Casarte, including network-enabled products like the first fibre-detecting washing machine.

Everywhere, digital screens and projectors fit seamlessly into wall panels and cabinets, activating as customers approach

PMT PARTNERS reinterprets classical symbols and forms in the context of modern commerce

Zhe Zeng

Left The space is partitioned vertically into three floors, with a two-floor atrium composed of concentric circles and ovals.

Above The design team sought to transform Jiamila's brand characteristics into spatial features, creating a space that is both sublime and inviting.

YIWU – The 430-m² flagship store for Islamic fashion brand Jiamila represents a translation of classical architectural vocabulary and embraces the label's relationship to religious faith. Guangzhou-based designers PMT Partners transformed the most deeply rooted character-istics of the brand into spatial elements that are not merely ornamental. The result is a space that feels simultaneously opulent and awe-inspiring, focused on the material and the immaterial.

Located in the centre of the commercial city, the flagship took over four pre-existing street-level shops. Once the partitioning walls had been demolished, the empty shell featured only one central structural column and cross-beam. These elements became the foundation of PMT's design concept and gave the team the free-dom to sculpt the interiors: To fulfil the brand's requirement of no less than 400-m² of display area, the space is partitioned into three floors. At the centre, a 9.5-m-high atrium was built around the symmetry created by the structural column and crossbeam. Its geometry, composed by concentric circles and ovals, encourages shop-pers to travel up to the second and third floors, effectively solving the stream of customers across the entire retail area.

PMT inserted a pendentive structure into the atrium that gives the space a pared-down but classical Byzantine look. The dome which would traditionally be supported by such a pendentive was replaced by a cylindrical structure that acts like a well of artificial light, completing the space's poetic – almost sacred – interior.

Left The atrium contributes to efficient traffic flow between levels, helping to draw visitors up to the store's second and third floor instead of losing them on the first floor's 100-m² display area.

Right Top Matte black, white and grey tones are accented with fields of burnished gold, recalling a Byzantine fresco.

Right Bottom The building's new framework, the pendentive structure and cylindrical light well, suggest the unmistakable quiescence and awe of a religious space, but of no particular era, place or faith.

Next Spread The original crossbeam is the root of the design, diminishing the stereotypical aspects of the dome and the pendentive so that the design reaches beyond a mere imitation of the classical to suggest something more profound and not merely formal.

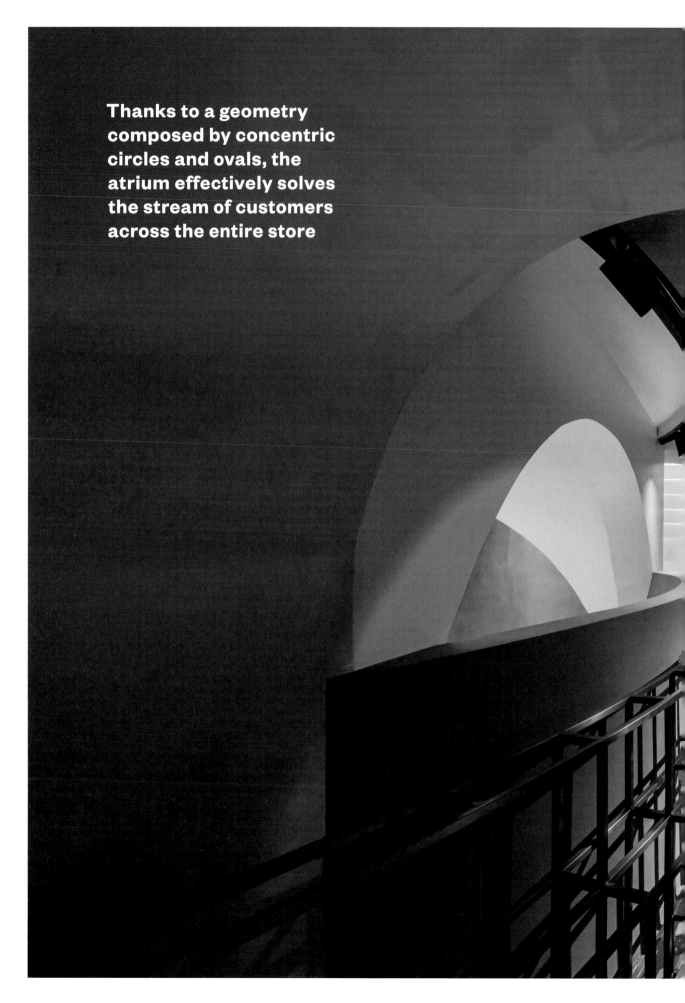

Thanks to a geometry composed by concentric circles and ovals, the atrium effectively solves the stream of customers across the entire store

GREATER DOG ARCHITECTS
highlights the craft of tailoring through spatial narrative

头部 Head
颈部 Neck
胸部 Chest
腰部 Waist
臀部 Hips
大腿 Max Thigh
膝盖 Knee
小腿 Calf

SHAOXING – For suit brand Leding Bespoke, Shanghai-based studio Greater Dog Architects reinterpreted the garment production process into the store's spatial narrative. Greater Dog founders Jin Xin and Red Hu were invited into the brand's production studio before the design process begun. Fascinated by the craft, the team brought artefacts like fabrics, patterns, thread, chalk, pins, irons, and even old sewing machines to the interior. These objects mark the start of a narrative which the designers hope ensures that the hand-making process, itself, is as intuitively apparent to shoppers as the suits on show.

Around the stairway entrance, a display installation – which showcases tailoring tools and products – consists of a cascade of 10x10-cm cubes that represent the time it takes to craft a bespoke suit from scratch. Customer circulation and the remaining zones, including body measurement, seating and fitting areas, are arranged around this 'Time Flow' installation. At the store's perimeter, garment racks are tucked into the walls while other wall displays are designed to mimic a 45x45-cm fabric catalogue cabinet.

Through an engaging spatial narrative, the design brings an old craft back into contemporary life, evoking the memory of hand-made processes while creating a successful retail space.

Rachel Wu & Red Hu

Previous Spread A 2:1-scale illustration of the male body is represented on the cobalt blue glass wall of the stairway entrance.

Left The blue and white interior tells the story of the tailoring process by creating opportunities to display both products and artefacts of the artisanal process within the retail space.

Above The space is organised around a central entry stairway clad in cobalt blue glass.

Right A model of the 'Time Flow' installation whose cubes serve as flexible display for products and tools of the trade, and a storytelling canvas.

Greater Dog Architects

Left Top Wall displays of suit components, shirts and colourful accessories mimic old fabric samples cabinets.

Left Bottom A long terrazzo table in the VIP lounge emphasises the geometric language of the space.

Right The architects composed an intuitively 'readable' space through illustrations of the body, measurements and the display of old tools.

The designers reinterpreted the garment production process into the store's spatial narrative

ARCHSTUDIO plays with reflections to create an infinite, exhuberant space for a multi-brand boutique

Previous Spread The design team adopted an intelligent lighting system throughout, embedding lights into mirror-clad spaces with a view to meeting the needs of different activities and settings.

Left Mainly functioning as a multi-brand boutique, the venue, which is available to rent, can accommodate a variety of activities, including exhibitions and dining.

Above One of three 'courtyards' in the building contains a staircase with sharply articulated steps flanked by a 6-m-high green wall.

BEIJING – For multi-brand store Mirror Garden, local design firm Archstudio renovated a small stand-alone building in a hutong, replacing its original flat roof with a pitched structure and integrating the volume into the surrounding built environment. Inside, the team interspersed crisp lines and monolithically white surfaces with vignettes of lush greenery and mirrors to transform the architecture into an infinite 'garden'.

A key element of the design concept, indoor/outdoor connections were established thanks to three small 'courtyards' which bring in ample sunlight and greenery. The first marks the entrance and leads visitors to the ground floor product display area. Here, mirror-lined walls and ceilings produce, in the designers' words,

'multiple reflections of people, objects, furniture and plants and generate an interactive relationship between the "real" and the "reflected".' The second courtyard, a glazed light well featuring a tree, further animates this space. Finally, the third courtyard boasts a 6-m-high green wall and a staircase leading to the attic, which hosts a kitchen and dining space. Two terraces capping the north and south sides of the first floor attic allow indoor activities to be extended outdoors.

The 283-m^2 space features additional display areas in the basement, where gleaming surfaces serve as the backdrop for products and continue the concept of infinite perspectives and playful interaction between visitors and objects within the boutique.

'Multiple reflections generate an interactive relationship between the "real" and the "reflected"'

MIRROR GARDEN   279   ARCHSTUDIO

Previous Spread Objects displayed in mirror-filled spaces produce playful interactions between consumers and products.

Left The stairwell zigzags from the basement display area to the attic's kitchen and dining space.

Right The kitchen and dining table are constructed with terrazzo, together forming an 'L' shape, which enables the close interaction between chef and diners.

Below By cladding the ground floor with mirrors and dispersing micro-gardens throughout, Archstudio created an infinity from the limited space and turned the architecture into an ever-changing 'garden'.

Hong Qiang

Wang Ning

MITHRIDATE

RSXS evokes the spirit of the times to create a swank concept store

SHENZHEN – Founded in 2018 by fashion designer Demon Zhang, Chinese haute couture brand Mithridate tasked RSXS with designing its first flagship. The 600-m² concept store was to be luxurious but unfussy, bare but intimate. The Guangzhou-based studio ticked all the boxes, putting forward an environment that embodies 'the spirit of the times'.

In a high-end shopping centre, the team devised an easily reconfigurable and hierarchical space that also looks and feels straightforward and practical. For example, they created a retractable wall anchoring the centre of the store that can be used to open the space up, but which, when closed, shelters a private area where VIP customers may browse through the garments in peace.

A black and white colour scheme is accompanied by unembellished but sculptural display pieces and furniture, like the cash desk, made in a translucent, blushing resin. In tones of white, the bright space features a glossy terrazzo floor, thick, coarsely finished table legs, and light membranes stretched across parts of the ceiling. Ranged with ample space to wander among them, matte black garment racks hung with clothing resemble exuberant plant beds in a masterfully planned garden.

Previous Spread RSXS's design for haute couture concept store Mithridate reflects the zeitgeist through a minimal, reconfigurable layout.

Left The impossibility of implementing certain changes in the high-end shopping centre location greatly restricted the design, a challenge which was ultimately overcome.

Right A series of dark metal, oval jewellery display shelves can fold into and out of the white wall, as needed.

Jayson Ku

Above The cool marble paint and resin details help to make the space luminous.

Right The resin displays compliment, soften and warm the black and white space.

Next Spread The store's entrance features an arching wall that frames a circulation path.

A black and white colour scheme is accompanied by unembellished but sculptural display pieces and furniture

IPPOLITO FLEITZ GROUP
translates the high quality of a cult Chinese liquor into visual sophistication

Left The interior features a combination of digital and analogue media to make the display more engaging.

Above The rippling metal mesh exterior alludes to the mountainous region where baijiu making began and gives the traditional drink a youthful and cosmopolitan appeal.

Left The store's interior is a refined mash-up of diverse patterns and textures, with furniture by both HAY and Zaozuo.

Right Circular mirrors hang at various angles from the ceiling, reflecting the diaphanous layers and mineral textures around them.

Plan The design team envisioned a floor plan featuring geometries that aren't common to the typical retail environment.

SHANGHAI – Baijiu, a versatile and increasingly popular cocktail spirit, has its origins in the difficult to reach mountainous province of Guizhou in southwest China. For Guijiu, a new brand of the traditional liquor, German firm Ippolito Fleitz Group ensured that both the inside and outside of its 120-m² flagship represented the geographical origins of, and meticulous production process behind, the Chinese spirit. Visually, the space also unites the long tradition of baijiu making and drinking with contemporary culture.

Certainly the customer journey begins outside. The design team built a 'building within a building', inspired by the overlapping mountain silhouettes of Guizhou to sculpt a modern, undulating exterior and a swank but youthful interior.

The space translates into an ensemble of chic materials and geometric forms the exceptional care with which the brand invests the production process: Every object and surface is crafted with precision, from marble floors and metal mesh ceiling to the anodised stainless steel tube wall system, which was also designed to recall the Guizhou mountains. These superimposed silhouettes boast a layered transparency and lend the space a sense of intimacy while welcoming exploration.

To complete a captivating customer journey, the interior combines custom digital and analogue media displays also developed by the designers.

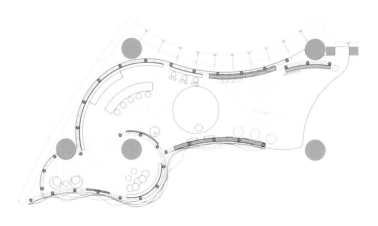

SHOWNI

U-GUIDE sculpts an artful and coherent display to increase the texture and depth of a retail floor

Above At the centre of the space (and the design concept), curved and undulating standalone walls envelope the main display area and successfully divide the store's functions without fragmenting the space.

SUZHOU – To make clothing boutique Showni stand out in a busy shopping street, design studio U-Guide created sculptural partitions and a high-contrast colour scheme, optimised display surface and added a little sleight of hand.

To increase square footage for visual merchandising without fracturing the space, the team constructed a series of partial walls by cambering the top edges of a ribbon stood on its side and then cutting it into four sections of varying length. By making the walls reach only part of the way to the ceiling, the designers were able to preserve the original height and visual openness of the room. The cuts establish asym-metrical 'doorways' and open an irregular route through the space that the designers call the 'punchline' of the interior design.

Marking this route, a strand of red air conditioning hose wafts and wiggles overhead, as if drawn by hand, helping to brighten and visually deepen the otherwise black, white and grey interior. It appears to float, but is actually suspended from the ceiling via transparent fishing line – a low tech effect that looks like magic and guides the customer's journey.

Shengsu Architectural Photography

Left On the left and right sides of the store, arched doorways frame garment display racks, adding to the overall style of the interiors.

Above The asymmetrical storefront distinguishes the shop immediately from the mall around it.

A strand of red air conditioning hose wafts and wiggles overhead, helping define the circulation path

Left Top Red display stands and transparent shelves made of acrylic further accent the interior.

Left Bottom A reception area and bar greet visitors entering the store.

Diagram The designers considered the plan and programme from two perspectives: from the front to the rear of the store, and from left to right.

Plan The design team was able to translate a typical fashion boutique layout – with clothing display taking centre stage and accessories display, dressing rooms and auxiliary areas occupying the back of the store – into a captivating interior.

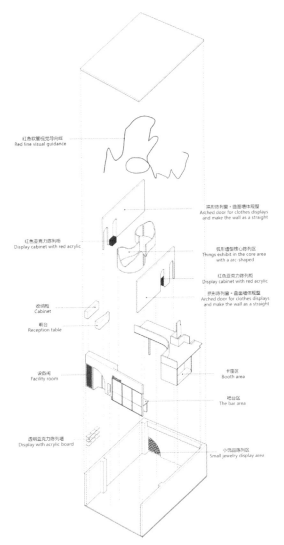

红色软管视觉导向线
Red line visual guidance

拱形陈列窗 + 曲面墙体规整
Arched door for clothes displays and make the wall as a straight

红色亚克力陈列柜
Display cabinet with red acrylic

弧形造型核心陈列区
Things exhibit in the core area with a arc-shaped

红色亚克力陈列柜
Display cabinet with red acrylic

拱形陈列窗 + 曲面墙体规整
Arched door for clothes displays and make the wall as a straight

收纳柜
Cabinet

前台
Reception table

设备间
Facility room

卡座区
Booth area

吧台区
The bar area

透明亚克力陈列墙
Display with acrylic board

小饰品陈列区
Small jewelry display area

尤格设计 U-Guide Architecture Design

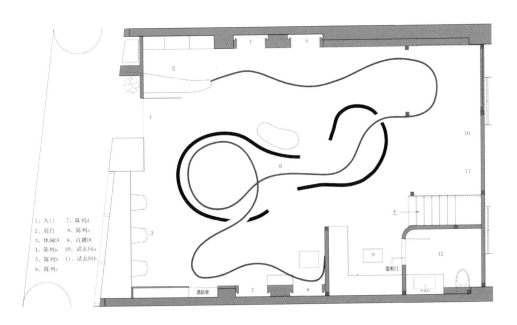

1、入口　　7、陈列d
2、前台　　8、陈列e
3、休闲区　9、直播区
4、陈列a　10、试衣间a
5、陈列b　11、试衣间b
6、陈列c

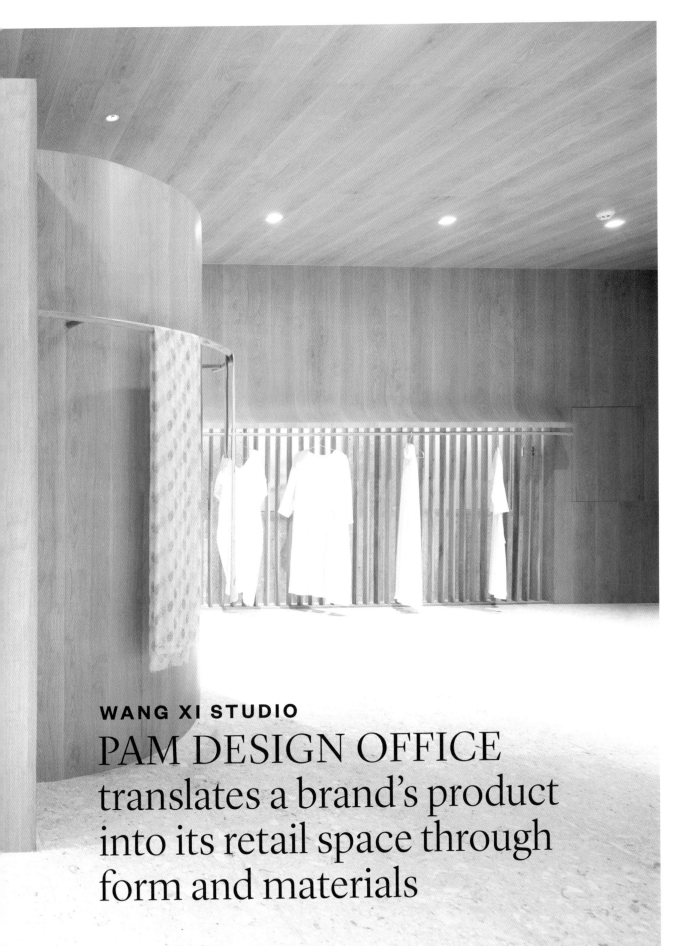

WANG XI STUDIO

PAM DESIGN OFFICE
translates a brand's product
into its retail space through
form and materials

Zhipeng Zhou

Previous Spread The meeting and tea break area is only partly enclosed and features a 'window' looking onto the display zone and entrance.

Left The store is divided into five parts according to its functional requirements: workshop, meeting room and break area, washroom, dressing room, and main display area.

Right The display area is contained in the 'skirt of the space' where the lower wall is rolled upward to expose a wooden grille as a frame for the garments.

Next Spread A cylinder is never just a cylinder, a straight line is never just straight; instead, PaM pairs distinct geometric forms in a way that echoes the structuring of a garment to the human body.

BEIJING – The interior concept for fashion boutique Wang Xi Studio had its origins in the brand's clothing. Taking textiles – their character, form and materiality – as the starting point, local firm PaM Design Office used wood seamlessly and profusely, establishing a consonance between the shop and the creative product that fills it.

Wood, a material whose textural and visual qualities the designers compare to those of textiles, envelopes the 81-m² store and integrates its various functional requirements. The display area is defined by an architectural 'skirt': At either side of the retail floor, the lower edge of the display walls have been peeled upward, like a lifted skirt, to expose the lower half of a grille made from elm wood.

Contrary to usual practice, a cylindrical dressing room occupies a prominent space in the interior, facing the store's main entrance. The meeting/ break room was placed in a semi-enclosed area, behind a half-height curved wall that partially separates it from the display area. It is, however, open on one narrow side and has a tall vertical cut-out through which staff maintain a visual connection with the entrance and display areas.

Completing the layout, a washroom and design workshop inhabit the most hidden area of the space. The creative energy of the latter, however, is brought back into the retail floor through architectural expressions integrated into the partitioning wall, like subtle vertical and horizontal openings.

Wood envelopes the store and integrates its various functional requirements

ZHUYEQING GREEN TEA
Product display takes a backseat to customer experience in a flagship by X+LIVING

CHENGDU – A 96-m² flagship store for green tea brand Zhuyeqing translates the language of traditional Chinese landscape painting into a modern retail interior. Shanghai-based studio X+Living took its cues from the 'cloud and mountain' motif common to the art of freehand ink painting – motifs that also allude to Zhuyeqing tea's place of origin, Chengdu.

The team recognised that product display no longer needs to be the focus of retail spaces, with customers conferring more value to spatial design and consumer experience. With this in mind, they looked to make the most of a small footprint by creating a rich sensory experience. The solution was to integrate function with aesthetics: Mountain and cloud-shaped modules rest on the floor, hang from the ceiling and rise from posts driven into the floor, forming a soft wooden landscape which hides and integrates a variety of functions, including sheltered seating in the open-plan space, product display, storage, and lighting.

The strategic organisation of 'mountains' and 'clouds' at different heights throughout the interior forms a path of circulation, contributing to the flowing, floating composition of the space. 'Walking in the space, as if traveling through the clouds, consumers can appreciate the interior at a leisurely pace,' the designers say.

Previous Spread The interior represents a modern interpretation of traditional Chinese freehand ink paintings.

Left The curved shapes hide a plethora of functional devices, from seating and storage, to lighting.

Below The integration of the store's functional and decorative elements allowed the team to make the most of a small footprint.

Shao Feng

The strategic organisation of 'mountains' and 'clouds' at different heights throughout the interior forms a path of circulation

Above The team borrowed classical motifs in Chinese landscape painting – mountains and clouds – to create the shapes of display surfaces.

Right Depending on their function, the modules are either entirely enclosed or feature open woodwork.

Plan The arrangement of the seating and display 'mountains' and 'clouds' was designed to define a fluid circulation through the room.

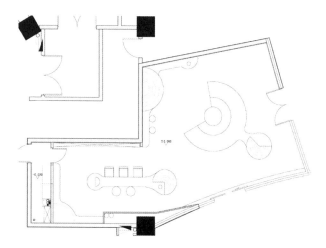

KEY TAKEAWAYS

As retail changes, mere product display takes a backseat to a space's capacity to enrich consumer experience.

In order to respond to the aesthetics of new consumer groups, retail spaces need to re-interpret traditional solutions through non-traditional designs. Interactive experiences and art installations are but two examples of the tools used by a growing number of designers.

In the age of click-and-collect, shops are starting to face inwards to heighten intrigue. But while kerbside presence is traded for concealment, inside the roles are reversed. The fitting room, previously tucked away in a hidden corner, now takes centre stage, becoming a backdrop for livestream shopping and retail theatre.

Digital media plays an increasingly important role in the creation of spatial narratives for today's retail spaces, but many successful customer journeys still rely on purely analogue solutions, through the creative manipulation of low-tech materials and spatial design.

DESIGNER INDEX

Mark Gong

Pan Shiyi

ALBERTO CAIOLA
Shanghai, China / Pordenone, Italy
albertocaiola.com
office@albertocaiola.com

Through his practice, Alberto Caiola
questions current design assumptions
and conducts research across disciplines.
Cross-pollination, disruption of expectations and visual storytelling lie at the
heart of the practice, allowing the team to
synthesise unique, authentic narratives
and then translate them into captivating
spaces. Unfamiliar combinations and
contradictions inhabit these projects,
plucking visitors out of their comfort zones
to immerse them in a new narrative and
the robust presence of materials.

P.030, 082

ANYSCALE
Beijing, China
anyscale.cn
office@anyscale.cn

Anyscale Architecture Design is an
international practice working to realise
its clients' dreams and deliver their
most ambitious goals. The studio's three
founders, Karin Hepp, Andreas Thomczyk
and Tom Chan represent a trio of diverse
personalities that nonetheless share the
same values and embrace the challenge
of designing at any scale necessary or
desired.

P.044, 136

ARCHSTUDIO
Beijing, China
archstudio.cn
archstudio@126.com

Since 2010, Archstudio has been creating
architecture in natural contexts, renovating and transforming urban architecture
and improving retail environments, advocating a balance between mankind and
nature, history and commerce. Archstudio
mediates relations between large and
small, new and old, interior and exterior,
artificial and natural, working to produce
environments that touch the mind and
elicit interaction between the space and
our behaviours.

P.274

ATELIER ARCHMIXING
Shanghai, China
archmixing.com
sc.mg@foxmail.com

Atelier Archmixing was founded by Zh
Shen and Ren Hao in 2009. Zhuang a
Ren were later joined by partners Tar
and Zhu Jie. The practice is known fo
innovative and flexible design strateg
which are rooted in China's complex
and rural contexts. Its work ranges ac
a broad spectrum of typologies and s
both domestically and abroad.

P.208

Yuuun Studio

.E. ARCHITECTURE STUDIO
g, China
e.net
o-l-u-e.net

ed in 2014 by Shuhei Aoyama and
uji, B.L.U.E. Architecture Studio
ternational firm whose name, an
m for Beijing Laboratory for the
Environment, represents its core
ophy. Focusing on the city's rich col-
f history with forward-looking cul-
e studio works across a spectrum
ologies, researching 'urban physics',
, culture and the environment.

COORDINATION ASIA
Shanghai, China
coordination.asia
pr@coordination-asia.com

Coordination Asia, founded and managed
by Tilman Thürmer, is an international
agency specialising in the design of
curated experiences and bold environments for museums, exhibitions and
brands. As a broad-spectrum design
consultancy, the agency provides a range
of services from the inception of a project
to its completion, from brand consulting,
curation, design conceptualisation to
detail design, realisation and supervision.

P.058, 164

DAS LAB
Shanghai, China
das-design.cn
mis@dasdesign.cn

Das Lab is an experimental studio led by
creative director Li Jingze. The practice is
devoted to exploring cutting-edge and forward-looking creative solutions for hybrid
businesses, culture, retail, and hospiatlity,
as well as unique world-class commercial
design. Das Lab has collaborated with
clients from diverse backgrounds such as
Holiland, Heytea, Mujosh, Starter, Vanke,
Longfor Group and LostVilla.

P.158

DAYLAB
Shanghai, China
daylab.cn
info@daylab.cn

Daylab was founded in 2013 by designer
Docee Dong to focus primarily on
behavioural research around improving
and updating commercial consumption.
The practice has gained a motherlode of
experience designing a new type of commercial interiors capable of integrating
online and offline retail. After several years
of development and growth, Daylab's
three partners are directing a team of more
than 40 designers.

P.040, 088

Shi Zheng

Gentle Monster

GQI ARCHITECTS
hai, China
qi.net
dong-qi.net

ed by Jiang Nan in 2014, dongqi
ects is a design practice dedicated
itecture, interiors, brand identity
eative content. The team combines
cal experience with the integration
ting-edge information technology.
7, dongqi established a creative arm
e the gap between architecture and
experience and to create space for
explore cross-disciplinary work in
stic manner.

E STUDIO
Shenzhen, China
estudio.guru
e-studio@foxmail.com

E Studio is a diversified creative consultancy founded by Xuanzhuo Zhou and
Junjian Fan and dedicated to exploring the
design of commercial space. The practice
excels in the use of cross-disciplinary
thinking in order to create a unique overall
identity for client brands and to address
business weaknesses from various points
of view. Services range from space, exhibition, brand and residential design, to
business research and multimedia design.

P.102

FUN UNIT DESIGN
Hangzhou, China
ifseeason@163.com

Zhu Xiaochen founded Fun Unit Design in
2015. The practice takes on commissions
in the fields of architecture, interiors,
installations and product design for clients
across a spectrum of disciplines and industries. Today, Fun Unit Design comprises
a team of 30 people. Its international
designers explore new creative directions
in the commercial market through an
experimental, narrative and humorous
approach to each project.

P.130

GENTLE MONSTER
Seoul, Republic of Korea
gentlemonster.com
cs@gentlemonster.com

Gentle Monster began life as a luxury
eyewear brand that rapidly earned
international recognition for remark-
able, ever-changing shop interiors and
art installations like its cuter-than-cute
dollhouse pop-up in Seoul's Sinsa district. Today, however, like the futuristic,
experimental SKP-S mall in Beijing, the
brand has begun to imagine wondrous
interiors for other businesses, as well.
Gentle Monster's masterful branding-
through-space is conceived in-house by
a 70-person interior design team.

P.186

GEOMDESIGN
Guangzhou, China
geomdesign.com
375661322@qq.com

Geomdesign was founded by Ye Guosu and Ma Yuzhao in 2018. The duo considers design a driver of business and brands. Their practice, which has grown into a 10-person team, represents a return to minimalist geometry whilst maximising the value of design. With each project they explore the value of space a little further, seeking to breathe new life into design and improve urban life.

P.154

Xinhui Guo

GREATER DOG ARCHITECTS
Shanghai, China
greater-dog.com
greaterdog@yeah.net

Founded by Red Hu and Jin Xin in 2015, Greater Dog's team of 10 architects, designers, artists and researchers is based in Shanghai and London. The avant-garde practice spans the fields of architecture, urban design, interior design, installation art, performance and architectural research in a spirit of experimentation and humanity, 'writing' architecture and space as a means of storytelling. The team employs performance and installation techniques to blur the boundary between commercial design and art, as well as to build a dialogue between people and spaces.

P.220, 268

I IN
Tokyo, Japan
i-in.jp
info@i-in.jp

Founded by Yohei Terui and Hiromu Yuyama in 2018, I IN is a Tokyo-based design firm that pursues new possibilities in the design of retail, office, hospitality, and installation space. With both the client and end-user in mind, I IN creates memorable environments that make a strong impression. The team finds original solutions by thinking outside of the architectural box, always working towards one main goal: sublime beauty.

P.248

IPPOLITO FLEITZ GROUP
Stuttgart, Germany
ifgroup.org
info@ifgroup.org

The identity architects at Ippolito Fl Group are all about pushing bounda through interior, architecture, produ and communication design. From it studios in Stuttgart, Berlin and Shan the team works with passion on solu that combine strategic expertise wit emotional intelligence, and create la value. Made up of 100 heads and he from a spectrum of disciplines, Ippo Fleitz Group makes each project uni As different as its tasks may be, the g is always the same: to create places t touch people's emotions, an approac highly valued by clients.

P.016, 024, 290

Anne-Sophie Heist

KCA
Shanghai, China
kcarchitecture.org
kostaschatzigiannis@gmail.com

Kostas Chatzigiannis leads eponymous architecture practice Kostas Chatzigiannis Architecture (KCA). The team's approach to each project involves exploring the possibilities of connection to and integration into the modern urban context. KCA is fascinated by materiality whether overseeing the renovation of a heritage building or creating a modern design that taps into the newest construction methods. During its 12 years, the firm has completed architectural and design projects at all scales.

P.200

KOKAISTUDIOS
Shanghai, China
kokaistudios.com
info@kokaistudios.com

Architecture and interior design firm Kokaistudios was founded in 2000 in Venice by Italian architects Filippo Gabbiani and Andrea Destefanis. Headquartered in Shanghai since 2002, it has grown into a multicultural community of 60 creatives, working on a global scale on cultural, corporate, commercial, hospitality and retail projects, as well as urban regeneration.

P.048, 118

KOOO ARCHITECTS
Tokyo, Japan
ko-oo.jp
kooo-contact@ko-oo.jp

Before founding Kooo Architects, Shinya Kojima and Ayaka Kojima worked in the office of Kengo Kuma & Associates on large-scale architectural projects such as China Academy of Arts' Folk Art Museum and Alibaba Taobao City in Hangzhou, and Sanlitun Soho in Beijing. The duo established Kooo Architects in Tokyo and Shanghai in 2015. Since then, a third office in Guangzhou opened its doors in the fall of 2019.

P.172

LANDINI ASSOCIATES
Sydney, Australia
landiniassociates.com
studio@landiniassociates.com

Landini Associates is a multidiscipli design agency globally renowned for work in food retail. Following a desig philosophy which centres on 'Reinve Normal', the team creates every cust touch point, from interiors to identit packaging and websites, uniform an print, in order to empower the cohes and powerful brands of clients like McDonald's, Esselunga, Loblaws an ALDI, among many others.

P.012

STUDIO
g, China
dio.cn
dio@126.com

udio's projects have been rec-
d internationally for the firm's work
ood, environmental performance,
hnological innovation. Founder
jie is committed to designing more
e, friendly spaces through creative
g, a spirit of craftsmanship and
nciple of caring for nature. Besides
g Luo Studio, Yujie also teaches
uction Basics in the School of
ecture at Beijing's Central Academy
Arts (CAFA).

MUR MUR LAB
Shanghai, China
murmurlab.cn
murmurlab@163.com

Mur Mur Lab was founded in 2016 by
designers Samoon and Lee. Their elegant,
minimal and atmospheric sensibility
places architecture at the core of design.
Focusing on retail and cultural space,
urban installations and micro-architectural
renovation, the duo sees design as a tool
for urban renewal and improving the
social environment. Mur Mur Lab is not
bound to tradition and is continuously
building surprises into everyday life.

P.224

MUUA DESIGN STUDIO
Huzhou, China
marketing@muua.com.cn

Yunfei Hua founded Rovvon Design in
2017. Two years later, the practice officially
joined the Muua Cultural Tourism Development as a partner, becoming Muua
Design Studio. Today, the growing team
consists of eight team members whose
focus remains on the field of hospitality
design.

P.106

NONG STUDIO
Shanghai, China
nong-studio.com
17nong@nong-studio.com

Nong Studio is a multidisciplinary
architectural design firm specialising in
commercial, residential and hospitality
projects that range widely across the
design spectrum from architecture and
interiors to furniture and graphic design.
The practice always works to create solutions that strike a balance between art and
design, as well as spaces that 'look back
into the future' whilst withstanding the
vagaries of time.

P.036

DESIGN OFFICE
g, China
esignoffice.com
ngqiang@pamdesignoffice.com

Design Office was founded by
qiang Mi in 2018. Today, the studio
own to six employees. The buildings
vironments envisioned by PaM are
ed to establish a fine, harmonious
e between function and experience,
e rooted wholly in the users' needs.
are solutions by which the studio
tirely re-imagine the potential of
pace.

PMT PARTNERS
Guangzhou, China
pmt-partners.com
pmtpartners@163.com

PMT Partners is an architecture and
interior design practice launched in 2016
and currently collaborating with clients
in China and around the globe. In an era
of precipitous and extreme change, lead
architects Yan Hu, Zhe Zeng and Weihao
Zhao take an open-minded and creative
but pragmatic approach to the work, creating projects that manage to be somehow
both radical and restrained.

P.262

RÅ SPACE
Changzhou, China
rahuset.com
info@rahuset.com

Visual designer Seamus Wang and
furniture designer Esben Yan founded
Rå Space in 2018 in order to pour fresh
energy into conventional home décor by
imbuing it with their own brand of Nordic
minimalism.

P.112

RAMOPRIMO
Beijing, China
ramoprimo.com
info@ramoprimo.com

Ramoprimo unites Italian and Chinese
architects to experiment with materials
and concepts. Founded by Marcella
Campa and Stefano Avesani, who have
been working between the two countries
since 2008, the practice focuses on
urban planning, architecture, interior
design and graphics. Its name refers to
a term Venetians use for certain hidden
streets and is the Italian translation of the
Chinese term Tou Tiao, the first lane in
a series of Hutong alleys in old Beijing.
The studio also participates in the Instant
Hutong project (instanthutong.com).

P.122

Xiaoyun

ROOMOO
Shanghai, China
roomoo.cn
info@roomoo.cn

Interior and spatial design studio RooMoo's approach to each project bears in mind the way the space will be inhabited and the context to which the space belongs. RooMoo's design ethos is underpinned by sophisticated architecture, innovative interior and product design, as well as cutting-edge graphics.

P.204

RSXS INTERIOR DESIGN
Guangzhou, China
rsxsdesign.cn
rsxs_design@163.com

RSXS Interior Design was founded by Jayson Ku in 2008. Working internationally, but with a focus on serving the Asia Pacific region and, in particular, its various fashion industries, the RSXS team focuses on creativity, diversification and regeneration. The studio takes on assignments that involve a range of branding experience, from space and brand vision system design to innovative brand image integration.

P.282

SIMPLE SPACE DESIGN
Zhongshan, China
dosign.lofter.com
dosign@foxmail.com

Tuno Liu founded Simple Space Design in 2017. Sanpin, the name of the office in Chinese, is derived from the pronunciation of 'simple' in English. Today, the practice consists of eight people, a team that is primarily engaged in the design of commercial space. Its work is based in the conviction that design can be used to improve the life of clients and make people happier.

P.094

SÒ STUDIO
Shanghai, China
sooostudio.com
info@sooostudio.com

Innovation-based architecture, inte and industrial design practice Sò Stu was founded in 2016 by Jessica Wu a Mengije Liu in response to a growing demand for the duo's distinctive des aesthetic, clever use of materials and thesis of imagination and intellect. S its inception, the studio has complet commissions that include restaurant retail space, workspace, galleries, pri residences, boutique hotels and cult institutions.

P.070, 182

SPACEMEN
Shanghai, China
spacemen-studio.com
explore@spacemen-studio.com

Founded by Edward Tan in 2014, Spacemen is an award-winning architecture and interior design office. With a team of internationally diverse creatives whom Tan describes as 'storytellers of space', the practice specialises in building a variety of brand architecture and environments. Capturing each client's unique brand strategies, culture and ideologies, Tan's Spacemen create one-of-a-kind spatial – and brand – experiences.

P.256

Chunhui Mo

STUDIO 10
Shenzhen, China
studio10.co
info@studio10.co

Founded in 2017 by Shi Zhou, Studio 10 is an interdisciplinary architectural design practice based in Shenzhen and with a branch office in Hong Kong. With an international perspective and a deep understanding of local culture, Zhou and her diverse team focus on creating bespoke, high-quality architecture and interiors.

P.240

STUDIO DOHO
Shanghai, China
studiodoho.com
info@studiodoho.com

Studio DOHO is a commercial interior design studio founded by Dutch designer Xin Dogterom and American Jason Holland with a simple premise: We create excitement. The studio specialises in hospitality, retail and office commissions, but always at the core of what it does is telling the story of each client. As licensed architects, the partners take a holistic approach to design, emphasising details, construction and project feasibility.

P.098

M2 Studio

SUPERCLOUD STUDIO
Shanghai, China
sc.mg@foxmail.com

Supercloud Studio is an 18-person m tidisciplinary design firm established 2010 by Xu Xunjun, Wang Yinghui a Yang Yuqing. Using design as a medi of connecting people to each other ar the environment, Supercloud strives improve social interactions in public and, by collaborating with artists and graphic designers, amplify the adapta of its work to local contexts and the a lives of its end users.

P.142, 208

Chu Lusi

Ema Liang

IDE
u, China
l.com
ign@yeah.net

X+LIVING
Shanghai, China
xl-muse.com
press@xl-muse.com

XIANXIANG DESIGN
Hangzhou, China
xianxiangdesign@163.com

XU STUDIO
Shanghai, China
xustudio.cn
xustudio@xustudio.cn

de Architectural Design Atelier
unded by Zhu Nianwei in 2013 in
Lumpur, Malaysia. In 2016, the
moved to Suzhou, China. U-Guide
mitted to providing excellent
solutions for quality living spaces,
focus on commercial, retail and
pace design.

X+Living, founded in 2011 by Chinese
architect Li Xiang, is an international
architectural design company in pursuit
of the perfect union of aesthetics and
functionality, art and pragmatism. The
firm's work ranges across industries from
hospitality, work environments and retail
to cultural space. In the conviction that
design creates value, Xiang insists on the
highest quality from concept through
completion.

P.306

XianXiang was founded in 2017 by
Yuan Lijun, whose practice explores the
limitless potential of immersive and
experiential spatial design through an
experimental design language. The studio
works on retail, business, hospitality and
other commercial projects, as well as
private residences and product design,
seeking to find balance in its use of form
and materials, and their relationship to the
context and users of the space.

P.194

Founded in 2016 by Yijun Xu and Shijin
Xu, XU Studio provides international
design services, including architecture,
interior and furniture design. XU's creatives believe that every project is unique
due to the singular nature of the client's
cultural context and branding strategy.
They conduct in-depth research into
materiality and the function, organisation
and flexibility of space, privileging user
experience over visual details.

P.176

N DESIGN
zhou, China
design.com
hi@163.com

ed in 2011, Yebin Design is an
r design practice working across
l typologies, from retail, hospitality
ork, to cultural spaces and high-end
nces. The studio is committed
ving the most forward-looking
ture-thinking clients, advocating
vity, collaboration, research and
strategy. The creative team believes
esign can deepen and even drive the
ercial value of space.

CREDITS

LEARNING FROM CHINA
A New Era of Retail Design

Publisher
Frame

Editor
Ana Martins

Authors
Shonquis Moreno
Ana Martins

Graphic Design
Barbara Iwanicka

Prepress
Edward De Nijs

Cover Photography
Wang Ning

Printing
IPP Printers

Trade Distribution Usa and Canada
Consortium Book Sales & Distribution, LLC.
34 Thirteenth Avenue NE, Suite 101
Minneapolis, MN 55413-1007
T +1 612 746 2600
T +1 800 283 3572 (orders)
F +1 612 746 2606

Trade Distribution Benelux
Frame Publishers
Domselaerstraat 27H
1093 JM Amsterdam
the Netherlands
distribution@frameweb.com
frameweb.com

Trade Distribution Rest of World
Thames & Hudson Ltd
181A High Holborn
London WC1V 7QX
United Kingdom
T +44 20 7845 5000
F +44 20 7845 5050

ISBN: 978-94-92311-49-8

© 2021 Frame Publishers, Amsterdam, 2021

The Koninklijke Bibliotheek lists this publication in the Nederlandse Bibliografie: detailed bibliographic information is available on the internet at http://picarta.pica.nl

Printed on acid-free paper produced from chlorine-free pulp. TCF ∞
Printed in Poland

987654321